M000100466

Latina Legislator

Leticia Van de Putte and the Road to Leadership

SHARON A. NAVARRO

TEXAS A&M UNIVERSITY PRESS

College Station

First edition

All illustrations in this book appear courtesy of Leticia Van de Putte

The paper used in this book meets the requirements
of ANSI/NISO Z39.48-1992 (Permanence of Paper).
Binding materials have been chosen for durability.

Library of Congress Cataloging-in-Publication Data

Navarro, Sharon Ann.
Latina legislator : Leticia Van de Putte and the road to leadership /
Sharon A. Navarro.—1st ed.
p. cm.—(Rio Grande/Río Bravo ; no. 13)
Includes bibliographical references and index.
ISBN-13: 978-1-60344-062-2 (cloth : alk. paper)
ISBN-10: 1-60344-062-3 (cloth : alk. paper)
1. Van de Putte, Leticia—Political activity. 2. Hispanic American
women legislators—Texas—Case studies. 3. Women
politicians—Texas—Case studies. 4. Hispanic American
politicians—Texas—Case studies. 5. Politicians—Texas—Case studies.
6. Legislators—Texas—Case studies. 7. Texas. Legislature.
Senate—Officials and employees—Case studies. 8. Texas—
Politics and government—1951– I. Title. II. Title: Leticia Van de Putte and
the road to leadership. III. Series.
F391.4.V36N38 2008
328.764'092—dc22
[B]
2008005211

To my parents, Vidal and Hope R. Navarro

CONTENTS

A gallery of photographs follows p. 84

ILLUSTRATIONS

(following p. 84)

ACKNOWLEDGMENTS

I first want to thank God for providing me with the words to write this book. I also thank my parents, who have supported me throughout my academic career. They made me the person I am today. My sisters, of course, are important to me. I thank my sister Faith, for reading earlier versions of this manuscript and providing important insight, and my sister Leslie, for helping me with the data collection early on and for being my confidante. To my brothers, Alex and Chris, thanks for your humor. There are others as well that I must thank, such as my dear friend Richard E. Martinez, who took time to read an earlier version and made extensive comments. Thanks to Rodolfo Rosales for reading an early version of the introduction and offering suggestions. Rachel Jennings has provided some valuable insight into this whole process. My dear friend Gaye Theresa Johnson: thank you. Valerie Martinez-Ebers and my anonymous reviewers: thank you. I thank Felix Alamaraz for his guidance regarding Texas A&M University Press. He is an invaluable source for junior faculty. I thank State Senator Leticia Van de Putte and her staff for their cooperation and patience. I thank my incredible research assistant James Zamarron. I also thank Mary Lenn Dixon at Texas A&M University Press for taking a chance on a junior faculty member writing about a Latina leader. And, finally, thanks go to my dear friends and family in Wisconsin, Michael and Linda, who always call to check in on me.

As I present this work to the public, I must emphasize that I take full responsibility for what finally appears in print.

Latina Legislator

INTRODUCTION

In May 1999, for the first time in its 150-year history, the city of Brownsville, Texas, elected a Latina[1] mayor. Blanca Sanchez Vela's decision to place herself in the mayoral race arose from the urgings of her family and the many friends and supporters she had won through her reputation as an activist while serving on boards and commissions in her community. Initially, Vela was reluctant, for, although she had lent her support to various political campaigns, she had never personally considered becoming a candidate; furthermore, it meant challenging the incumbent, a Mexican American man who had held the office for eight years. On the other hand, she believed that Mayor Henry Gonzalez was out of touch with the families of Brownsville; she was convinced she could do better. With her family and friends enthusiastically declaring their support, Vela knew there was no turning back. She campaigned for an entire year before the election. In her words, she wanted the people of Brownsville to "really get to know her."[2]

At a Rotarian luncheon held weeks before the election, Vela's status as a wife and grandmother was disparaged by her male opponent during the presentation of their individual campaign platforms before the audience. Noting with pride that she had served as chairwoman of the city-owned utility board for eight years, prior to which she had served as a bank board member for sixteen years, and before which she had been a housewife raising three children, Vela mentioned that she was now a grandmother. In his response, her opponent observed that "it takes more than a housewife and a grandmother to be mayor in this city." Angered, Vela countered: "I don't understand him . . . He's a grandfather himself. How does being a grandmother make me less qualified?" Following the incident, Vela's supporters wore T-shirts bearing a new campaign slogan: "Housewives and grandmothers can be mayors."[3] Vela ultimately defeated the incumbent, winning 56 percent of the vote.

In 1998, Elizabeth "Betty" Flores became the first Latina mayor of Laredo, Texas, in 240 years. Re-elected in 2002, Flores is also the first Mexican American woman mayor of a major city along the U.S.-Mexico border.

Betty Flores had a twenty-eight-year career in banking behind her. Hired as a secretary, Flores worked her way up through the ranks to become the first female to serve as senior vice president in Laredo National Bank's 106-year history.[4] Prior to her appointment as senior vice president, Flores had worked extensively in the business development section of the banking business, during which time she became increasingly involved in the community of Laredo. When she finally left the banking business, Flores worked for a community organization called the Aztec Economic Development and Preservation Corporation, a nonprofit that constructs and rents housing for low-income families in Laredo. It was through her involvement with this organization that Flores first became interested in politics. Working as an advocate for community development, she began to learn about the needs of the community.

In an interview with Sonia Garcia, reflecting on her decision to run for the mayoral office, she recalled an agreement she made with her husband when they were first married: "We promised each other that we would never go into politics . . . anything else would be okay." She described the moment when she decided to run for office: "One day we [she and her husband] were watching television and we learned that one more guy [had] announced his candidacy for the mayor's office, and so my husband turns to me and says, 'What's going to happen to Laredo?' So, I just let that thought pass for a while and then I turned to him and I said, 'What do you think about me running for mayor?' And he turned to look at me with this look on his face and he said, 'You know, I have been thinking the same thing.'" It was at this point that Flores knew she could win. While campaigning for mayor, Flores remarks, she never made any promises; rather, she was very "up front" with the people, constantly reminding them, "What you see is what you get." In 1998, in a special runoff election, the community of Laredo responded by electing her mayor with 55.39 percent of the vote.

In American society, running for elected office represents the ultimate act of political participation. Much of the literature on women in politics suggests that many who have successfully made that jump, like Vela and Flores, may not initially have considered themselves viable candidates. The literature also suggests that women are neither recruited by political parties nor groomed to be candidates: the training ground for women is the work they do in other peoples' campaigns.

To date, only a handful of scholars have published works on the subject of Latina elected officials. Very few studies exist to inform our understanding of how and why Latinas become political candidates and leaders. We do not know, for instance, what compels them to run, how they win (and win re-election), or even whether their race, ethnicity, or gender is a factor in their decision to run or their victories. All the existing research up to this point on Latina political behavior suggests that Latinas are *accidental leaders;* they are community activists or untraditional politicians who do not follow the typical paths or motivations that lead white males to politics.

Texas State Senator Leticia Van de Putte represents Senatorial District 26, nestled in the heart of San Antonio, Texas. The second Latina ever to serve in the State Senate, Leticia Van de Putte was a pharmacist and mother of six before making the decision to enter the political arena as a candidate. Even then, she was an accidental player rather than an ambitious seeker of political office.

Seventeen years ago, Leticia Van de Putte regularly volunteered in Democratic candidates' campaigns, with no thought of becoming an elected official herself. But when opportunity knocked, she accepted the challenge. Winning a special election in 1999, Van de Putte became only the second Latina in the history of Texas to win a seat in the Texas State Senate. In her first term as state senator, Van de Putte made a strong impression; in 2003, she led the walkout of eleven senators, breaking a quorum and thus halting senate business, an accomplishment that garnered her unprecedented media attention.

Indeed, Van de Putte is best-known in Texas politics as the leader of that forty-five-day walkout, staged by state senate Democrats in protest of a congressional redistricting plan backed by then-U.S. House Majority Leader Tom Delay (R-TX). The successful walkout notwithstanding, the Republican-controlled legislature ultimately adopted the new congressional map, which led to a gain of six Republican congressional seats in the 2004 election. On June 29, 2006, the U.S. Supreme Court upheld most of the congressional map, but ruled that changes to a district reaching into San Antonio discriminated against Latinos. The court said Republicans who drew the map discriminated against Hispanic voters in San Antonio's District 23 by diluting their voting strength, in violation of the Voting Rights Act.[5]

Today Leticia Van de Putte is one of only four women, and only two Latinas, in the Texas State Senate. In 2006, Van de Putte assumed the presidency of the National Council of State Legislatures (NCSL) from one of the nation's Republican strongholds, Texas. President of the NCSL from 2006 to 2007, she is the first Texan as well as the first Hispanic woman ever to chair the organization. The NCSL is an effective and respected advocate for the interests of state governments before Congress and federal agencies, providing research, technical assistance, and opportunities for policymakers to exchange ideas on the most pressing state issues.

From her very first race in 1991 (which she ran on a shoestring budget of just 56 dollars, defeating five male candidates), Senator Van de Putte has yet to lose an election or re-election bid. She has become one of the most politically powerful Latina policymakers in the Texas legislature.

The aim of this book is to deepen understanding of the behavior of Latinas as políticas. State politics have become increasingly important as arenas of policymaking, and very often serve as a training ground for higher office. My study illuminates the experiences of women of color in the Texas state legislature. Van de Putte provides a rich case study of how Latinas can achieve positions of political prominence, and of the significant repercussions that attend this hard won prominence.

While studies of women in politics are not lacking in the literature, very few focus on women of color in elected office. There are numerous studies focusing on the pathway to elected office for white women, but very few analogous studies for Latinas. My work both uses and challenges conventional research in the field of Latino politics by providing an in-depth analysis of a highly male-centered process, first showing how a little girl from the west side of San Antonio could become one of the most powerful Latinas in state politics, and then asking how gender influences this process. Can women succeed on their own terms? Are they simply women playing a man's game according to men's rules and objectives, or are female politicians actually reshaping the game? Is Van de Putte representative of a new generation of Latina politicians who have gone beyond mere tokenism? Obviously, answers will not come easily in the short space and time we have here, but hopefully the questions raised will afford us insights into how this particular Latina fared, and whether she has made a significant difference from a gender perspective.

Organization of the Book

This book is divided into seven chapters. Chapter 1, "Theorizing on Texas Politics Today: Looking Back," provides an overview of Texas politics. Beginning with a discussion of the state's political culture and parties, this historical context is useful in understanding the lack of female, and particularly minority female, representation in the state. I also equip the reader with a general understanding of the legislative branch, the functions of committees and chairmanships, and the dearth of female representation in these powerful bodies.

The following chapter, "A Theoretical Understanding of Women in U.S. Politics," provides a review of the literature on women in politics beginning with political socialization, which is the combination of factors that determines whether women become candidates (that is, political ambition and the structure of political opportunity). Against this backdrop is highlighted the limited understanding of Latinas as political candidates and the significance of the contribution of my study to this field.

Chapter 3, "The Early Years: Biracial Marriage and Political Maturation," chronicles the life of (then) Leticia San Miguel from childhood to adulthood, and on to her marriage to Henry "Pete" Van de Putte. The purpose of this chapter is to familiarize the reader with Leticia's political socialization and political participation; herein we get a sense of the struggle Latinas face between fulfilling cultural expectations and challenging them. As expected, the degree of her political participation changed following her marriage.

The next chapter, "Making the Connection between Politics and Community," contextualizes Van de Putte's pathway to her first political office in San Antonio. The findings in this chapter appear to be consistent with existing literature on women candidates. It documents her frustration with the lack of a strong political party, to winning the party's primary seat in 1991 against all odds, to her decision to run for the state senate.

Chapter 5, "Symbols and Substance: Theorizing about Latinas Leading the Legislature," explores the literature on legislative representation; specifically, the importance of maintaining what Hardy-Fanta called community *connectedness* through symbolic legislation, such as resolutions, is examined.[6] In this chapter I compare Van de Putte's legislative productivity directly to that of the other Latina women who were elected and served in the Texas State Legislature while she was a member of the House and Senate. Scholars contend that for Latino and Latina representatives, maintaining a symbolic connection with constituents through legislative resolutions contributes to reelectability. Moreover, as the literature on women in politics reveals, this is precisely what makes a female legislator more effective in the eyes of her constituents.

The following chapter, titled "*The Illusion of Inclusion* Revisited," examines Van de Putte's rise to positions of leadership within the state legislature, her ability to persuade eleven state senators to break quorum in protest over the Republican effort at redistricting, her rise to prominence in various national organizations, and what all this means for Latina state legislators. The walkout alone made her one of the most politically powerful Latina leaders in one of the most entrenched "good ol' boy'" institutions in Texas, the state legislature.

Lastly, chapter 7, "Looking Forward," discusses the Texas state legislature in the postredistricting era and theorizes about the future of Latinas as *políticas* in Texas. This chapter identifies the ways in which Van de Putte represents a new generation of Latina leaders, and addresses the future of Latina elected officials in the state of Texas.

ONE

Theorizing on Texas Politics Today

LOOKING BACK

RECRUITING WOMEN into politics, like recruiting men, depends upon a number of factors that influence each phase of the recruitment process—namely, eligibility, selection, and election.[1] The literature on women in politics suggests that a potential candidate's decision to seek office depends upon the political culture in which she finds herself, which either denies or provides opportunities to eligible people.[2] The potential candidate must calculate whether to risk nomination by taking into account the closed or open nature of the relevant political structure. The purpose of this chapter is to identify the critical sociopolitical factors associated with opportunities for women's recruitment to the Texas state legislature. The two factors this chapter examines are political culture, reflected in institutional structures and membership, and the history of political parties in Texas. These two factors will give us an indication of the degree of diversity in representation.

Context of Women in State Legislatures

A handful of studies have attempted to answer why women of color do not experience higher rates of representation in state legislatures.[3] Scholars contend that women of color are often overlooked as political elites, which results in a striking lack of published research on elected officials who are women of color.[4] Researchers have proposed the standard gender model[5] as the most accurate predictor of women's presence in state legislatures. In other words, there is a general consensus within the literature on women and politics that the strongest indicators for predicting women's state legislative office-holding are a combination of (1) state features, including general population characteristics, political cultures, and liberal political ideologies, (2) legislative factors such as multimember districts, part-time legislatures, and term limits, and (3) an eligible pool of potential candidates. However, the literature is conspicuously silent on the issue of how race or ethnicity might affect this standard gender model. This gap in the equation is why Leticia Van de Putte's election to the state legislature deserves attention. By taking a closer look at Van de Putte's political socialization, we can think about how other Latinas might win elected office in a conservative southern state, despite what the literature on women in politics dictates.

Political Culture

For years historians and political scientists have struggled to identify the nuances that distinguish the political cultures of states. Daniel J. Elazar, a political scientist, defines political culture as "the historical source of such differences in habits, concerns, and attitudes that exist to influence political life in the various states."[6] As the embodiment of society's attitudes and values, political culture defines the rules by which an individual must play in the political process. Political culture can account for the many factors that make up a group of people who are distinctive in the way they talk, the way they act, and, of course, in the way they approach politics. Research has shown that Americans are socialized to believe that politics is men's work and not an appropriate pursuit for women.[7] This bias in the American political culture can arbitrarily "limit women's personal development, social choices, and opportunity to share fully in the dominant values of the society."[8]

Texans embrace an outlook on politics and government that is part southern, part western, and wholly unique. Throughout this book you will find evidence that Texas is, in fact, just as the Texas

Tourism Board says, "Like a whole other country."[9] We can gain insight into Texas politics with the help of Elazar's 1972 identification of the three predominant political cultures in the United States—moralistic, individualistic, and traditionalistic—an identification that is widely accepted by political scientists today.[10]

Borrowing Elazar's theory of political culture, David Hill systematically tests the hypothesis that state political cultures are important determinants of female representation in the state legislatures. Hill suggests that Elazar's "traditionalistic" and "moralistic" political culture may be related to female representation in state legislatures. For example, in traditionalistic cultures female participation in legislative politics is apt to be discouraged by elite opinion leaders who seek to maintain a male-oriented status quo. Conversely, moralistic political cultures are "receptive to the values and style that have been associated with women—concern with the public welfare rather than personal enrichment and so forth."[11] From the perspective of democratic theory, Hill concludes that political cultural is substantially more influential than structures such as political parties, redistricting, and institutional requirements in determining female presences in the state legislature. His study also seems to indicate that the traditions and historical patterns of some states may cause female representation to lag behind popular support for women's full participation in political affairs.

Elazar describes the political culture of Texas as a mix of traditionalistic and individualistic. As we shall see, the hybrid nature of the political culture in Texas is reflected in its institutions, with ramifications for the representation of women therein.

The Texas Legislature

In order to understand how structural constraints can affect a woman's decision to run for office, one must first have an overview of the legislative institution. As the lawmaking branch of the government, the Texas legislature assumes a certain primacy in the state's political scheme. After all, before the courts can interpret the laws and before the executive branch can put laws into effect, someone has to create them. Actions taken by the legislature touch virtually every aspect of Texans' lives, from public health and safety to education, and from criminal justice to the environment. The legislature, in essence, oversees a multibillion dollar "corporation" by virtue of the fact that it approves the state's biennial budget.

Article 3 of the Texas Constitution specifies that the Texas legislature must be a bicameral body, meaning that legislative power is vested in a two-house assembly, the Senate and the House of Representatives. The Senate, called by some people (mostly its own members) "the upper house," is composed of thirty-one people, the House of Representative 150. Both figures represent the maximum for each chamber allowed by the constitution. The legislature meets in regular session for not more than 140 days every two years, beginning in January of odd-numbered years. It is considered a part-time legislature because it meets for only five months. Other meetings of this assembly, referred to as *special sessions,* may only be called by the governor, are limited to agenda items determined by the governor, and may last no longer than thirty days. It should be noted that there is no limit on the number of special sessions a governor may call.

The structure of the Texas legislature clearly reveals the suspicion with which the authors of the constitution viewed government, in general, and lawmaking bodies, in particular. Created to handle the political business of a sparsely populated, largely rural state in the late nineteenth century, this body was designed to do its job, then get out of town. Although Texas has since become one of the largest, most complex urban states in the nation, that same attitude prevails today: For 19 months out of every 24, legislators pursue their careers and live somewhat normal lives (albeit with a fair amount of intrusion from the legislature). Then, for five months, convening in a gigantic political and governmental pressure cooker, they attempt to govern a monster with a budget of $57 billion a year. More than anything else, it is this severe time constraint that shapes the people of the Texas legislature and what they do.

Membership

The citizens of the state elect members of the Texas legislature in partisan elections. Members of the House of Representatives serve two-year terms, with no limit on the number of terms a representative may serve. To serve in the House, a person must be a U.S. citizen and a registered voter, reside in Texas two years prior to election, reside in the district one year prior to election, and be at least twenty-one years old. The official salary for members of the legislature, whether they serve in the House or Senate, is set by the Texas Constitution at $600 per month or $7,200 a year, as well as a per diem of $125 during both regular and special sessions. This low salary, coupled with missing 140 days every two years from work (not counting special sessions), makes it difficult for anyone to serve as a state legislator.

Senators are elected to four-year terms and they, too, have no limits on how many terms they may serve. In order to ensure some degree of membership continuity from session to session, one half of the Senate is elected every two years. The exception to this rule occurs after each decennial reapportionment, when all Senate seats are contested. Following such an election, lots are drawn to determine which fifteen senators will serve two-year terms. For example, Leticia Van de Putte was first elected in a special election to the Senate in 1999. She went up for election during the regular election cycle in 2000 and won. She drew the lot to run for reelection in 2002 and 2004. Since she drew the two two-year cycles, she will not be up for reelection until 2008. In order to serve in the Senate you must be a U.S. citizen, a registered voter, a resident of Texas for five years prior to election, a resident in your district for one year prior to election, and at least twenty-six years old. Senators receive the same salary and the same per diem allowance as House members.

Up to now, we have examined the structural factors that affect women's political recruitment and electability to the state legislature. The critical context of political culture, which defines attitudes concerning who ought to participate in politics, and the institutional nature of the legislature also affect women's candidacies. We next turn to the question of political parties in Texas politics.

History of the Democratic Party in Texas

According to Wilma Rule's work on women's legislative recruitment, a state's political culture is not the only barrier to a woman's electability. Rule maintains that states dominated by Southern Democrats pose unfavorable political climates for women in politics. Why? Such states have a nonegalitarian heritage. They have traditionally restricted women's political and social roles, rejecting both women's suffrage and the Equal Rights Amendment. Potential women candidates for southern legislatures have to overcome sex-role biases.[12] Add to this the influence of Spanish and Mexican cultural expectations on women of Mexican descent: a woman's role is as a wife and mother and does not extend outside household duties. In former times, Mexican American women never took on leadership roles in political parties. Instead, they served as organizers: working the phone lines, making the copies, and other "background" tasks. These roles were enforced by the conservative nature of political parties; these women never challenged their traditionally expected gender roles. Over time, the expectations of women with respect to political parties have changed. Accordingly, a review of the history of political parties in Texas is merited.

The Democrats were one of the first political parties to organize in Texas, formally establishing themselves in 1854. They dominated the political scene, although they occasionally saw challenges from the dying Whig party and the secretive Know-Nothing party during the 1850s. And, although the issue of secession divided Texas Democrats, it did not tear them apart as it did the national party. When Texas did secede in February 1861, most officeholders who took the new oath to the Confederacy were Democrats, and this pattern continued throughout the course of the Civil War.[13]

During Reconstruction, virtually anyone who had held office in either the Confederate or state government was barred from holding further office, and most were disenfranchised, with the result that Republicans held the majority of elected offices during this period. Only in the early 1870s were former officeholder's rights to vote and hold office restored, but once this happened, they returned with a vengeance. By 1873, in reaction to the perceived excesses of Reconstruction, most Republicans had been routed from office; for the next hundred years, the Democrats, for all practical purposes, were the only game in town.[14] The fact that there was only one viable political party in Texas after Reconstruction does not mean there was no political competition: Democrats fought other Democrats for political dominance. Mexican Americans had to battle their way into the Democratic Party's structure.

Prior to 1972, each state elected two members of the Democratic National Convention (DNC), one man and one woman. In Texas, they were the handpicked representatives of the governor. In 1972, the Texas DNC delegation took on a new face. No longer was the state represented only by the governor's representatives, but also by others who reflected various elements of the Democratic constituencies—blacks, Mexican Americans, liberals and Wallace conservatives. Joe J. Bernal (Van de Putte's *compadre*) of San Antonio was elected from the McGovern Caucus, and for the first time, Mexican Americans were represented on the DNC. Under the McGovern Rules, states are required to give proportional representation to presidential preference caucuses and primary candidates that capture at least 15 percent of the vote.[15] This was essentially the party's way of changing the old "winner-take-all" system. In December of 1975, a few concerned Mexican American Democrats (MAD) decided that it was time to formally create a structure through which to make positive inroads and gains within the Democratic Party. The group grew out of a conflict over the selection of state delegates to the 1974 Democratic Mini-Convention in Kansas City, at which just four of the ninety-six Texas delegates were Hispanic. DNC member Joe Bernal and other Mexican Americans described this as an act of discrimination and asked that five Anglo (Caucasian) delegates be replaced with Mexican Americans.[16] Starting in 1976, MAD held annual conventions and lobbied for the adoption of pro–Mexican American positions by the larger Democratic Party. In 1978, the first Latina, Sylvia Rodriguez of San Antonio, was elected to participate in the DNC, because of her work with Joe J. Bernal, then Texas state senator, from 1967 to 1972. She would serve until 1984.[17]

During her term, the Hispanic Caucus teamed up with the Black Caucus to write the bylaws that would insure that the chair of each caucus would automatically be a member of the executive committee of the DNC, where all the decisions were made. These rules are still in place today. (At the national level Rodriguez used the word "Latino" as an inclusive term to include mainly, but not exclusively, Puerto Ricans and Cubans. The name "Hispanic Caucus" also denotes the inclusivity inherent in the term "Latino.") Rodriguez worked to institutionalize Latino membership in the executive committee of the DNC. Because of their positions in the DNC, Bernal and Rodriguez constantly fought for the inclusion of Mexican Americans into the state Democratic Party. In 1982, the constitution stipulated that the chairman and vice chairman of the organization be of the opposite sex. The purpose of the organization was "to seek full representation of Mexican Americans at all levels and in all activities of the Democratic Party, taking appropriate public stands on issues relevant to our communities; and proposing, supporting, and when necessary, opposing legislation relevant to the Mexican American community."[18] In 1985, the DNC Executive Committee revoked official recognition of the Hispanic Caucus to deflect accusations made by the Republican Party that the Democratic Party was being run by "special interests." The caucus still exists, but it no longer receives support services from the DNC. The group still has its vice-chairs, as well as ex-officio membership on the DNC Executive Committee.[19]

The Democratic Party has been and continues to be an obstacle for Mexican Americans and, in particular, Mexican American women, for two reasons: First, the Democratic Party continues to take the membership of Mexican Americans for granted. Moreover, with its long history of dominance, the "Democratic Party assumes that Latinos are naturally Democrats and believe that they do not have to look for candidates because there are always enough Latinos interested in running."[20] Over the years, the Republican Party, however, has made serious strides in actively recruiting Latinos. Second, the Democratic Party, much like the Republican Party, has historically existed as enclaves of male dominance.[21] That is, neither party actively recruits women, provides male endorsements of women, or funds them as candidates.[22] It might not be entirely surprising, therefore, that other studies on women's election to office argue that gender bias and overt sexism in the recruitment process (when one even exists) have contributed to women's underrepresentation.[23]

Diversity in the State Legislature

It is important to examine the demographic makeup of the legislature in order to gain a better understanding of its aggregate membership. One obvious measure of its internal composition is party affiliation. As of 2007, the House of Representatives contained 81 Republicans and 68 Democrats. The Senate numbered 20 Republicans and 11 Democrats. These totals represent the second largest number of Republicans in the legislature (the first being the 2005 legislature) in more than one hundred years, and the GOP majority in both houses (the second since Reconstruction) is historic. These new realities clearly indicate the ascendancy of the Republican Party in Texas politics.

The diversity found in Texas as a whole is not as readily apparent in the legislature. The membership tends to over represent middle- and upper-income groups, while relatively few so-called "working Texans" (people with "8 to 5" jobs or people who punch a time clock every day) are found among the legislative ranks. The largest single professional group among legislators has always been lawyers. Business is also well represented in the legislature. The popular (though unfounded) notion that only lawyers can create laws may account for the predominance of lawyers, and a desire to protect the climate in which their businesses operate might explain that of businessmen.

Yet the predominance of these two occupational groups may also be due to that key element we mentioned earlier—time. Lawyers and businesspeople, who have more control over their own schedules, especially if they are in some kind of partnership, are more likely to adapt to the "full-time, part of the time" nature of the legislature. It is unlikely that people who must work on a regular basis would seriously consider legislative service.

Few studies have examined the role of women in Texas politics.[24] Despite all the rhetoric that surrounded the "year of the woman" in 1992, women in Texas experienced less than average status in the 1990s compared with women in the other forty-nine states. In an earlier study, Janet Boles contends that despite the fact that Texas has produced a number of prominent female politicians, the reality is that women's political participation in Texas falls below the national average.[25] As Boles points out, Texas women have acquired an image of the "archetypal" Texas woman in politics. Drawing from the rugged, individualistic tradition of the Western frontier woman, a mythology has surrounded Texas women such as Barbara Jordan, Ann Richards (and more recently U.S. Senator Kay Bailey Hutchison and the former Texas comptroller and Independent gubernatorial candidate, Carole Keeton Strayhorn). Sue Tolleson-Rinehart and Jeanie R. Coleman Stanley examine the initial success of Ann Richards in 1990.[26] As the authors posit, the 1990 gubernatorial race between Ann Richards and challenger Clayton Williams symbolized how gender affects voters' behavior. The author's analysis reveals that Ann Richards's victory was a result of a unique combination of characteristics. She was tough enough to convince voters that she could lead and feminine enough to put them at ease about electing a woman to a powerful position. At the same time, she remained committed to the progressive and women's issues that had won her the early support of feminists and progressives. Ann Richards epitomized the challenges women often face as candidates in Texas. She also provides an archetype of the successful female Texas politician.

Coleman Stanley's research on Texas women candidates found that in 1994 a record number of women sought office, particularly at the statewide level; the author notes that a total of twenty-one women ran for statewide or congressional office.[27] Yet their rate of success (43 percent) trailed that of men (54 percent). Equally important, it was Republican women that made the greatest gains, reflecting the national and statewide trend towards Republicanism. This trend was further solidified in 1994 with the election of Republican George W. Bush and the defeat of Governor Ann Richards. One should note that the 1994 gubernatorial election was one of the closest in Texas history; Republican women candidates clearly rode in on the coat-tails of Republican candidate, George W. Bush. This trend has continued from 1996 to the present in statewide judicial and legislative elections.

Over the past thirty years, the Texas legislature has slowly begun to mirror the state's ethnic mosaic. It is still, however, predominately composed of white, protestant males between thirty-five and sixty years of age who were born in Texas.[28] The seventy-eighth legislature that convened in January of 2003 included twenty-eight Hispanic and fourteen African American members in the House.[29] This session of the legislature also witnessed the swearing in of the first Asian American House members, Representative Martha Wong (Houston) and Representative Hubert Vo (Houston).[30] The membership of the Senate included seven Hispanic and two African American members. Gains in minority legislative seats are attributable in large part to the use of single-member districts since the 1970s. Although encouraging, these numbers still lag behind the overall percentages of each group in the general population. Moreover, recent federal court rulings questioning the constitutionality of the race-based apportionment schemes of 2003, together with the 2002 Republican landslide, were not welcome developments for those who sought to increase minority representation in the legislature.

Compared to the 1990 census, the 2000 census reveals a dramatic trend toward greater cultural diversity in Texas. Over the ten-year period, the Anglo majority declined from almost 61 percent to 52.4 percent, while the percentage of Hispanics increased from 25.5 percent to 32 percent, and the rapidly growing "Other" classification (primarily Asian, Pacific Islanders, Middle Easterners, and Native Americans) grew from 2.1 percent to 4.2 percent. The African American percentage of the total population remained relatively stable, moving from 11.7 percent to 11.6 percent.

More startling is the discrepancy between the legislature and the general population with regard to gender. According to the Center for American Women and Politics, of the thirty-one members of the Texas Senate, there are a total of four women. Out of a total of 150 members in the Texas House of Representatives, thirty-two are women.[31] The number of females in both state houses has slowly increased over the last ten years.

According to the National Association of Latino Elected Officials there are 2,137 Latino elected officials in Texas.[32] In the Texas State Senate there are a total of seven Latinos. Of those seven, five are male and two are Latinas. In the State House of Representatives there are 29 Latinos, seven of whom are Latinas.[33] If we were to go back as far as 1991, we would see that the number of Latina state legislators has reached a plateau (see appendix 1).

Women have made substantial gains in achieving elective office in the United States over the past several decades. Despite these gains, women, especially women of color, are still greatly underrepresented in comparison to their proportions in the general population.[34] However, scholars have noted that women of color served at higher rates than women in the aggregate, and white women in particular.[35] In 2007, 1,733 of the 7,382 state legislators in the United States are women. Women currently hold 422 of the 1,971 state senate seats and 1,311 of the 5,411 state house or assembly seats. There are 1,733 women state legislators serving nationwide, 344 of whom are women of color. These include 93 senators and 251 representatives. Women of color constitute 4.7 percent of the 7,382 total state legislators.[36] Of the 1,733 women state legislators serving nationwide, 71 are Latina. As of 2007, Texas was ranked 27th out of 50 states for percentage of women elected per available seat, with 36 women out of 181 state legislators. Nine Latinas serve as state legislators in Texas, with two of the nine in the state Senate.[37]

In the state of Texas, the number of Latinas elected to the state legislature at any one time has remained fairly constant. At the time Leticia Van de Putte was first elected in 1990, a total of five Latinas had been elected to the state legislature. In 1992 and 1994 there were nine Latinas elected, followed by ten in 1996, eight in 1998 and 2000, and nine in 2002.

It was not until Judith Zaffirini's election to the Senate in 1986 that Texas would see its first Latina elected to the state legislature since becoming a state in 1845. The second Latina to ever serve in the state legislature was Leticia Van de Putte, in 1999. Despite the institutional and political cultural barriers, Latinas, much like any other minority in Texas, have struggled to have their voices heard in the state legislature.

Methodology

With qualitative research, generalizability is always a question. This study was based on an examination of personal correspondence, state documents, personal records, campaign material, video transcripts, interviews, and secondary sources from 1990 to 2007 concerning Texas State Senator Leticia Van de Putte, and the legislative records of other Latinas. Van de Putte provides a rich case study of how Latinas can achieve positions of political prominence and why this hard-won prominence has significant repercussions. This methodological approach makes "a basic assumption . . . that the meaning people make of their experience affects the way they carry out that experience."[38] I use what Anselm Strauss and Juliet Corbin call "grounded theory," meaning, "theory . . . derived from data, systematically gathered and analyzed through the research process."[39] In this method, the researcher does not begin with a preconceived notion but rather "allow[s] the theory to emerge from the data" so as to offer insight and enhanced understanding of the phenomenon in question.[40]

Yet some may question the validity of those insights. There are at least four reasons why I believe my findings will contribute to the study of Latina politics. First, scholars such as Luis Fraga and others[41] suggest that Latina state elected officials are uniquely positioned to leverage the intersectionality of their ethnicity and gender in ways that can be of strategic benefit in the legislative process. Although Fraga's study of strategic intersectionality (via a quantitative analysis of bills introduced and issues supported) makes a major contribution to the field of Latinas in politics, the study does not provide an understanding of how Latinas achieved political prominence and what Latinas bring to policymaking and politics. This is a consistent gap in the literature on women, particularly Latinas, in politics. My examination of these conditions through a case study analysis will allow us to theorize about future Latina political candidates.

Second, David Hill suggests that state political cultures are important to understanding female representation in state legislatures.[42] Given Texas' unique political culture, where the number of Latino representatives is disproportionate to the state's largest ethnic group, Latinos, it is important to understand how Latina women can become significant leaders in one of the most male-dominated institutions, the State Senate, in one of the most conservative states in the country, Texas.

Third, attention to the role of gender and ethnicity or race in the electoral process, and more specifically to the presence of women among elected officials, is critically important because it has implications for improving the quality of political representation. Because of their minority status, Latinas bring to their elective office significantly different experiences from their white female, white male, and minority male counterparts. My study examines the impact their presence has had on governance and the legislative process. Their effects are in fact "indelible"[43] and cannot be erased from the face of Texas politics. And, finally, this study makes a contribution to the small, but growing body of literature on Latina elected officials in Latino politics.

TWO

A Theoretical Understanding of Women in U. S. Politics

Of the numerous studies that have examined the factors affecting women's election to public offices, most reveal no aggregate bias in society against women.[1] Controlling for partisanship and incumbency, women are just as likely to be elected as men.[2] But these studies do not provide a full picture of why the number of women in office is far lower than that of men, why women are more likely to be elected to some offices than to others, and why women in one location are more likely to be elected than their female counterparts elsewhere. To address these questions, political scientists have begun to focus on the various environments in which female candidates are recruited and elected.

As early as the publication of Maurice Duverger's seminal work, *The Political Role of Women* (1955), scholars have investigated why more women are not elected to office, and in order to do so have examined many things, including the kind of women who run for office, the role political party leaders and other political elites play in encouraging or discouraging women to run, and the geographic, political, and cultural environments most conducive to promoting women's candidacies.

Most women who hold public office in the United States do so at the local level—as opposed to the state and national levels, where elected women are still considered something of a novelty. However, most studies of female candidates focus on races for state legislative and congressional seats. So the question arises: How does a

Latina living in Texas, one of the most conservative of the southern states, make the leap from candidate to elected official? I suggest that Leticia Van de Putte made the leap by behaving like a strategic politician, not only in winning her first election to the Texas State House of Representatives and eight years later the Senate, but also in leading the Texas Killer D's to Albuquerque, New Mexico, in 2003 to protest the redistricting efforts of state Republicans.

Scholars such as Gary Jacobson and Irwin Gertzog have identified the characteristics of a strategic politician and examined the influence this type of politician can have, once elected to Congress. Similarly, Luis Fraga and others have argued that Latina elected officials are uniquely positioned to leverage their ethnicity and gender in ways that can be of strategic benefit in the legislative process.[3] Those scholars have examined the strategic politician following elections; my study looks at the making of a strategic politician.

Socialization

To understand women in their role as potential candidates, we must first examine the socialization patterns of women. The most obvious manifestation of traditional gender socialization is a woman's role in her family. Examining the political socialization of Latina women, Hardy-Fanta found that the family (either an already politically active family, or the support of family while running for office) is the most important contributing factor in their political development. While Latinas face barriers to political participation stemming from sexism and cultural traditions, their political participation is "inextricably linked with the development of the political self" and "evolves in conjunction with personal self-development."[4] In other words, as they become more politically active, Latinas experience personal growth and become more politically aware. In her examination of twenty-nine Latinas in Boston, Hardy-Fanta found a common theme among these women: there is process, as she puts it. For some, it is a contemplative and slow process of awakening political consciousness; for others it is sudden, "a quick *chispa*[5] of recognition that a change is needed."

Hardy-Fanta identifies some of the major sources of political socialization for Latinas. Some Latinas reported that coming from a family tradition or background of cultural beliefs that values "helping others" had a major impact in their politicization process. As Baca Zinn observes, moving into politics allows Chicanas and Latinas to escape their traditional sex roles, and promote Chicano culture at the same time.[6]

Traditionally, women's familial responsibilities have limited their ability to participate fully in politics. Male and female candidates often differ in their familial responsibilities, with women having the greater number of private commitments. Thus, when a conflict arises between political ambition and family, women tend to choose in favor of their families, whereas men more often choose their ambitions. Virginia Sapiro and Barbara Farah suggest that women's roles in the family and at work can have either a positive or negative influence on the development of political ambition.[7] In particular, the presence of young children in the household makes it more likely that women will delay or even forgo their political aspirations.[8]

Hardy-Fanta also finds that some of the Latinas who have become politically active have undergone a kind of "countersocialization" as adults, a reorientation or transformation that challenges the expectations put on them by society, the culture of women, or the culture of Latinas. In other cases, rather than being a source of support, the family is actually part of the oppression that drives Latinas to become politicized. In still other cases, it is the traditional roles of Latinas as caretakers and mothers that are ultimately the stimulus for their politicization. Overall, Hardy-Fanta concludes, the process of becoming politically conscious for these Latinas is the process of "making connections—between their own lives and those of others, between issues that affect them and their families in the neighborhood or community and those that affect them in the workplace."[9]

They make connections between the private sphere of family and home and the public sphere of politics.

Another factor affecting socialization is gender-role perceptions, or, as Cynthia Enloe prefers, gender psyche.[10] According to Enloe, gender psyche refers to the phenomenon in which women and men are taught to accept different roles in politics. Women, for instance, are more likely to have lower political aspirations than men because they are taught by society to view their roles differently. Consequently, some have argued that women who have experienced a countersocialization are more likely to seek office.[11] Countersocialization usually takes place later in life, when the woman is an adult, and provides an experience that fundamentally alters her attitudes and beliefs about women's ability to participate in politics.

Women Becoming Candidates

Before turning to my case study of Van de Putte's initial decision to run for office, I would like to establish my investigation's theoretical underpinning, which has its base in the literature on women in politics. Studies have documented the *relevance of gender* in various aspects of campaigning.[12] Most studies focus on the rate of success of women candidates in congressional races. For instance, the National Women's Political Caucus, in their study of congressional candidates from 1972 to 1992, found that success rates were almost identical for men and women: in open seats, women fared no differently than men. Similarly, Gaddie and Bullock, in their study of gender in open seat outcomes from 1982 to 1992, found that women won seats in much the same manner as men, that is, they had elective experience and access to adequate financial resources.[13] In effect, when women won the party nomination (as they did in record numbers in 1992) they were usually elected to Congress.

Studies have been mounted to evaluate the reasons for the continued underrepresentation of women in elective office. Some of these studies focus on the *electoral opportunity structure,* meaning those long-term conditions, external to the individual, that affect both the demand for candidates and candidates' ability to achieve official positions.[14] As mentioned in chapter 1, among the factors that make up the electoral opportunity structure is the party context, the political context, and the social context.[15] The party context refers to internal party conditions (such as party rules concerning the representation of groups when considering candidates) or general party ideology, which can affect the degree to which a candidate is viewed as attractive. More specifically, issues such as recruitment by party elites, disparity in political resources (such as fundraising), the incumbency effect, and voter discrimination, are all examples of party context. Recent studies suggest that women have largely overcome these barriers.[16] Discrimination by party elites has diminished. Women are competitive with men with regard to fundraising, and voter hostility toward female candidates has declined. In sum, these studies suggest that "when women decide to present themselves to the public as candidates for local, state, and national offices, their chances of winning are as good (and sometimes better) than those of men."[17]

What remains is the social eligibility pool and expectations about the candidate's background and experience. Darcy, Welch, and Clark, for instance, find the "eligibility pool" to be the culprit for the relative absence of women as political candidates. Studies presented by Thomas and Wilcox and Garcia and Marquez show that women are less likely to come from traditional avenues of political office, and are more likely to have entered politics from community volunteerism or women's groups.[18] Because women have different backgrounds and credentials, they are less likely to view themselves as viable candidates.

Women are also considered, using Gary Jacobson and Irwin Gertzog's terminology, *strategic politicians*. These scholars use the term to examine the potential influence this type of politician has, once elected to Congress. Gertzog demonstrates how women who present themselves for election and win seats in the U.S. Congress are politically experienced, skillful, resourceful, and rational in their office-seeking calculations. The hegemonic model that emerges from

Gertzog's study reveals politically ambitious women adapting to or being transformed by institutional norms, rather than the reverse. Strategic women, by definition, are ambitious and skilled, qualities that are necessary to achieve power in Congress.[19]

Similarly, Luis Fraga and others examine the strategic intersectionality of Latina state legislative officials. They argue that Latina elected officials are uniquely positioned to leverage the intersectionality of their ethnicity and gender in ways that are of strategic benefit in the legislative process. These researchers argue that the combination of substantive policy focus (that is, focusing on policy of particular interest to working-class communities), multiple identity advantage (that is, the ability to build cross-group coalitions that provide legislative support), and the gender inclusive advantage (softening their ethnicity by promoting themselves as women, mothers, and community advocates) results in strategic intersectionality.[20] Using the framework provided by these researchers, I argue that Leticia Van de Putte, in winning her first election to the House and Senate and successfully leading the Texas Killer D's to Albuquerque to protest the redistricting efforts of Republicans in 2003, epitomized the characteristics of a strategic politician.

The particular qualities that go into making a strategic politician were identified from an examination of the literature on political recruitment and legislative elections. First and foremost, strategic politicians are ambitious. Their principal goal is to win public office, and, once there, to use lower levels of office as springboards to higher office. They are also unlikely to be "conscripted" by party leaders to run in hopeless elections unless doing so does not require them to give up the office they presently hold. In such a case, the decision to exploit a losing campaign is made calculatedly, in order to position themselves for a more promising future contest. Strategic politicians are also unwilling to allow themselves to be "co-opted" by party leaders, should they enjoy a celebrity status.

Strategic politicians are skillful and resourceful, articulate, and present an appealing physical and temperamental image. They conduct effective campaigns, carefully selecting relevant issues on which to capitalize. Their networks of friends and supporters tend to be extensive and diverse, enhancing their ability to cultivate and maintain the loyalty of both state and local party leaders. When combined with a formidable ability to attract financial support, these features have a tendency to inhibit serious opposition in primary elections.

Those who qualify are also experienced, professional politicians. They already hold (or have recently held) public office when they seek higher office. Occupying office allows them to establish rapport with constituents, and gives them experience in dealing with state and local bureaucracies. Strategic politicians tend to be task-oriented professionals, who realize that future victories depend on verifiable claims of legislative achievement. Knowing this, they publicly take responsibility for policy change and policy reinforcement. Successful campaigns for lower office help them develop the confidence they need to seek higher office.

Finally, strategic politicians are calculating and rational. The chances of their securing their party's nomination are carefully considered, and entry into a race is based on the likelihood of success. They calculate how victory or defeat will affect their careers, and, more often than not, wait for an incumbent to retire or otherwise take leave of absence before seeking that office. Political decisions, particularly those about whether to run and which office to seek, are made dispassionately, and only after the advantages and drawbacks of each course of action are subjected to rational analysis.

Latinas in Politics

Most of the literature on gender and politics does not take into account the experiences of women of color, especially Latinas. What limited literature there is on Latinas calls attention to the "triple oppression" faced by this group. This type of oppression includes racial, sexual, and cultural traditions that encourage or perpetuate passivity, submissiveness, and strict gender roles.[21] Fraga and others apply this premise to the concept of strategic intersectionality. As Montoya, Hardy-Fanta, and Garcia point out, the literature on

Latino politics contains few, if any, works devoted to women's political participation and leadership.[22]

Takash also notes the lack of attention paid to Latina electoral activism. Part of the problem is that scholars tend to dichotomize politics into either representational or grassroots politics. To fully understand Latina political participation, researchers must recognize that there is a connection between grassroots politics and representational politics. Furthermore, they must acknowledge electoral activism as a vehicle for accessing political institutions, as well as a means to bring about fundamental social change. Latinas, in particular, draw links between these various political arenas.[23]

In their closely related study of Latina party activists, candidates, and officeholders, Garcia and Marquez found that, far from being monolithic, Latinas have a variety of reasons for becoming politically involved, garnered from a combination of traditionally relevant political motivations and specific community-oriented motivations. That is, politically active Latinas exhibited a commitment not only to getting particular candidates elected and certain policies addressed, but also to their immediate communities and to the larger Chicano or Latino community as well. In effect, it was found that Latinas are entering traditional mainstream politics armed with their experience in grassroots politics, as well as with their cultural networks and resources. Moreover, participants voiced a wish to "see others like themselves involved in politics." These added dimensions render Latinas and Chicanas unique in mainstream politics and point the way to a more robust and complex understanding of the reasons why people become politically active.[24]

Hardy-Fanta, as mentioned earlier, concludes that, as candidates, Latinas must be able to view politics and participation "as making connections."[25] These connections might involve connections between people, connections between private troubles and public issues, and connections that lead to political awareness and action. It is through these connections that Latinas, unlike Latinos, reflect a more participatory vision of politics that incorporates cultural needs and expectations. Pardo, in her study of the mothers of East Los

Angeles, contends that Chicanas are able to transform traditional networks and resources based on family and culture into political assets.[26] Takash, in her study, contends that Latina political officials in California are able to overcome barriers of race, class, gender, and culture largely because they are able to draw from their experiences as long-time community activists. Takash found that over 61 percent of California public officeholders "include community activism in their descriptions of their political experiences" and over 68 percent had participated in political campaign activity prior to their first elected or appointed position.[27] Jose Angel Gutierrez and Rebecca Deen also note that the Chicano Movement of the 1960s and 70s provided Chicanas with experience of and exposure to the power structure. In particular, La Raza Unida Party, as well as numerous organizations such as MAYO (Mexican American Youth Organization), provided Chicanas with access to political opportunities.[28]

Studies have shown that when only one candidate is a member of a racial or ethnic minority, and particularly if no candidate from that racial or ethnic group has ever run before, it has the effect of generating enthusiasm and galvanizing turnout among minority voters.[29] However, when two or more candidates are members of racial or ethnic minorities, the issue of race and ethnicity may not necessarily play a central role.[30]

Culture and ethnicity are also relevant in campaigns involving Latinas. In her study of Latinas in the Boston political scene, Hardy-Fanta refers to a factor she calls *personalismo* as being significant for Latinos and Latinas in electoral politics. In effect, Latino electoral politics means "face-to-face, personal contact rather than impersonal, quick messages." What's more, she finds that Latinas make references to personal, face-to-face contacts during mobilization efforts more often than Latinos. As Hardy-Fanta notes, this observation ties in with feminist literature, which ascribes a "relational" point of view to women, in which women attempt to link the individual to family, friendship networks, and community relationships.[31]

Despite the *personalismo* factor, the barriers and obstacles facing Latina candidates are many. Some commented that they are often "pigeonholed" as representing only the needs and concerns of Latinos; others reported that their activism in local Chicano organizations was sometimes used as a weapon against them, with which to attack their views. According to Garcia and others, Latinas had their competency called into question. In 1998, during a mayoral debate, Blanca S. Vela, in her bid against the male incumbent for mayor of Brownsville, was asked about her lack of elective experience. She responded by saying, "I came from the volunteering field, not the political field. I want[ed] to be mayor so that I could listen to the elderly [and] to the young people; this is what I've done. I've walked South, North, East and West Brownsville. My goal was to do as much as possible so people could see someone cares about them."[32] Vela emphasized her connection to the community and her eagerness to improve the quality of life for the people of Brownsville.[33]

Gender stereotypes also impact Latinas. As cited in Witt, Paget, and Matthews, former National Women's Political Caucus (NWPC) president Irene Natividad points out, "Minority women must establish themselves as 'credible candidates.' They must be able to raise money and be encouraged as candidates."[34] Similarly, assessing her own campaign in 1990, California congressional candidate Anita Perez Ferguson, a former president of the NWPC, felt that her gender and ethnicity affected her candidacy because minority women must work harder to establish their credibility. She was quoted as stating that the general perception is "not one of competency and leadership."[35] As Gutierrez and Deen note, some female candidates had their husbands campaign for them "to assure male voters that the women would be capable of treating men fairly, especially in cases of domestic and child support."[36]

Another important challenge for Latina candidates is the responsibility they feel for their own families and children. It is not uncommon for Latinas "to express feelings of guilt, of neglecting their parental and familial duties, even when their children are grown but remain at home."[37] Many of the Latina public officials in California had children under the age of eighteen, making child care a big concern. In many cases, these women had to coordinate child care arrangements. Equally important, cultural traditions expect the full support of their spouses and family. In another study of Texas county judges, it was found that age, family size and obligations, cultural bias, marital status, and economic disadvantage can all serve as barriers to women seeking public office. In addition, the authors found that a lack of political resources, especially when facing incumbents, played a factor in the experiences of Chicanas seeking election to county judgeships.[38]

In 2003, a symposium sponsored by the Eagleton Institute of Politics with a focus on Latinas as candidates found similar results. The panelists, who included Dr. Christine Sierra as well as organizations such as HOPE (Hispanas Organized for Political Equality) and MANA, A National Latina Organization, concluded that among the formidable challenges facing Latinas are the lack of a pipeline—that is, particular professions in the private sector, such as law and business, that traditionally lead to political office—a lack of role models, the need for campaign financing, and the need for campaign experience and skills.[39]

Women Leading the Legislature

Why is it important to have women in roles of legislative leadership? Why is Leticia Van de Putte's leadership important? The literature on democratic theory emphasizes the values of equality and representation in policymaking institutions. Mansbridge argues that having women in positions of leadership in the legislature not only fulfills the democratic ideal of equality and representation, but also translates into tangible benefits for other women legislators.[40]

Three schools of thought address the issue of leadership. The first points to the effects of traditional socialization in family and work roles. According to Valian, girls and women are more likely to learn, practice, and be rewarded for cooperative behavior than are boys or men.[41] Hochschild suggests that sex-segregated work tends to reinforce and perpetuate gender styles learned from family and other childhood experiences.[42] Jamieson contends that the media perpetuate images of women as professional caregivers, self-effacing volunteers, or submissive partners to prominent men.[43]

The second school of thought speaks to psychological orientation effects. Carol Gilligan's research suggests that gender differences stem more from psychological development than from socialization, and result in differences in moral "voices." According to Gilligan, women embrace the ideals of responsibility, caring, and connectedness.[44] This view is consistent with Takash's findings concerning public officeholders in California, in which Takash found that Latina representatives practice "a politics of difference"; that is, the author noted that while Latinas support feminist agendas, they "express more concern with issues facing the Latino community as a whole, such as employment, access to education and retention in school, and safe neighborhoods, issues largely stemming from institutionalized racism and classism."[45]

The third school of thought arises out of studies based in the private sector, outside of political science; that is, women employed in managerial positions that are less top-down, less controlling, more inclusive of others, and more open to the sharing of power and information. Helgesen contends that women, more than men, emphasize spending time with people, caring, being involved, and helping others.[46] Furthermore, Eagly and Johnson found that both interpersonal relationships and task accomplishment are emphasized by women to a greater extent than by men.[47] Jewell and Whicker found that women leaders were more likely than men to adopt a "consensus" style, and much less likely to adopt a "command" style.[48] Based on a study of state legislature committee chairs, Rosenthal presents evidence that women place greater emphasis than men on involving citizens, providing opportunities for others to participate in the decision making process, listening to others, and seeking consensus.[49] In a later work, Rosenthal also reports that, in terms of conflict resolution strategies, women chairs are more inclined than men to collaborate and to accommodate the concerns of others.[50]

Legislative leadership is often conceptualized as either symbolic or substantive. Chapman defines symbolic legislation as "legislation sponsored with the objective of giving psychological reassurance to constituents that representatives are working in their interest and are responsive to their needs."[51] This kind of representation is purposive action designed to further the interests of someone. Beyond providing visible evidence that a legislator is working on behalf of his or her constituents, a legislator can produce tangible outcomes by advocating for an issue, which is known as substantive representation. This is the more common type of representation and the type that constituents expect.

However, there is evidence that some symbolic representation is necessary. For instance, Jane Mansbridge argues that symbolic representation actually enhances substantive representation.[52] Chapter 5 profiles state senators like Leticia Van de Putte, who are very much aware of this fact. Van de Putte is perceived as one of the most responsive legislators in San Antonio, Texas, and has not had a serious challenge to her office since her first election in 1991. Comparing Van de Putte's legislative record to the other Latinas who served with her in the House and the three other women in the Senate, her record of symbolic legislation is almost equal to that of her substantive legislation. This is critical for minority representatives, because it demonstrates that they are able to foster trust and facilitate communication between themselves and their constituents, lending legitimacy to governing institutions. Perhaps more importantly, symbolic legislation reflects the interests and concerns of the constituents. Finally, symbolic representation allows for the crystallization of interests, which is necessary for substantive representation.[53]

While remaining concerned with constituent representation, women also tend to have a broader legislative focus because they see themselves as representing women in general, a phenomenon Susan Carroll terms "surrogate representation."[54] Thus, so-called women's issues (those issues pertaining to women, children, and family) place high on the list of legislative priorities.[55] Women representatives share the experience of being female, a mutual experience that gives them a broader sense of the female perspective than their male counterparts, and results in a heightened awareness of, support for, and commitment to feminine issues.[56] They are in a unique position to articulate and be responsive to "women's" interests in a way unavailable to their male counterparts. In effect, their symbolic similarities have substantive implications.

Women and Committee Assignments: A Review of the Literature

One of the most important institutions in the legislature, whether at the federal or state level, is the committee. There is a plethora of literature on committees at the federal level, but very little with regard to committee assignments in the various states. The committees women are placed on can determine how much power they have in policymaking. As such, a review of the existing literature is important to establish a general understanding of women and committees.

As Sinclair argues, "The distribution of valued committee positions provides the single best observable indicator of the distribution of influence in Congress."[57] Committee assignments are an indication of the institutional power base from which a senator operates and are crucial to a senator's prospects for playing a significant role in policymaking. The positions held by a member of Congress are critical in defining his or her career as a legislator.[58] At the federal level, the "Big Four" are the prestige committees: Appropriations, Armed Services, Finance, and Foreign Relations Committees. The Armed Services and Foreign Relations Committees are viewed as prestigious and powerful because they provide a platform for national recognition and an opportunity for important international policymaking. The Appropriations and Finance Committees derive their prestige from the "power of the purse": they control spending and taxing, respectively. In performing this duty, both committees reach deep into national and international policymaking.[59]

Beyond an analysis of the institutional value of the committee assignments lies a consideration of the breadth of interests encompassed by women. As Noelle Norton and Debra Dodson have demonstrated, in order to have a voice in policymaking, sitting on a committee with jurisdiction over an issue is very important.[60] Increasing the number of women in the Senate should, by definition, increase the representativeness of the Senate. However, in one possible scenario, the committees to which women are assigned may be more closely associated with women's issues, leading to a higher level of representation on these particular issues, and precluding representation on a broader range of issues. If women are concentrated in particular areas based on beliefs about their expertise, or because they are given typical freshman assignments on less-substantive committees, then enhanced representation across all issues may not be achieved at the committee level.

The literature on women in elective office suggests that the presence of women in the legislature is important in order for the legislature to address women's issues. For instance, Arturo Vega and Juanita Firestone found that women legislators' voting behavior and introduction of bills led to an increase in the representation of women's issues.[61] Other studies also indicate that the presence of female legislators is likely to increase the introduction of legislation pertaining to women's issues.[62] However, the addition of new women does not necessarily enhance female representation on committees that address these "women's issues." The diverse jurisdiction of many Senate committees means that these issues may fall under the purview of more than one committee, and, for the same reason, women's issues may make up only a small fraction of the agenda.

According to Duerst-Lahti, women serve on a wide variety of committees in the Senate. They are not concentrated in areas associated with women's issues, although they are clearly represented on these committees.[63] The achievement of breadth in committee assignments has substantive implications for representation. Women senators are represented on all major Senate committees, including five on Appropriations and two on Finance, the highest-ranking committees.[64] Such wide representation is a substantial feat, especially from an institutional perspective, wherein it is understood that a senator's effectiveness is influenced by the power he or she holds within the institution. Representational breadth also provides all women senators with an opportunity to introduce a female viewpoint into a variety of policy debates, a situation only bolstered by the influx of new women and by the increasing seniority of those previously elected.

As Mansbridge and Tamerius assert, the institutional power that comes with more prestigious committee assignments further supplements the substantive representation already achieved through the representational breadth found in Senate committees.[65] Committee and subcommittee positions are even important for those interested in participating in policies of salient interest to women, such as abortion, family planning, and welfare reform.

Summary

The purpose of this chapter is to familiarize the reader with the literature of women in politics. To understand the experiences of Latina elected officials, one must first understand the experience of women in general. Latina experiences are different from Anglo women's experiences and it is important to identify the differences. I begin with a discussion of women's socialization process, then proceed to a discussion on women as candidates, as legislative leaders, and then as committee members. Moreover, this chapter offers a theoretical framework that draws from the previous research of Jacobson, Gertzog, Fraga, and others by suggesting that Leticia Van de Putte has matured into a strategic politician. No other study provides us with an in-depth analysis of how she has become one of the most powerful Latina players in Texas politics today. A closer look at her political maturation is warranted.

THREE

The Early Years

BIRACIAL MARRIAGE AND POLITICAL MATURATION

LETICIA'S POLITICAL SOCIALIZATION had a lot to do with the influence of her mother and extended family. They instilled in her a strong sense of self and independence. The character of Leticia's mother is best understood by looking at the life experiences of Leticia's parents.

Leticia Van de Putte's mother, Isabelle "Belle" Ortiz, was born in 1933 in San Antonio, Texas, to Lupe Aguilar and Roy Aguilar.[1] Lupe was from Guadalajara, Mexico, and Roy was from Seguin, Texas. Belle was born in Santa Rosa Hospital and raised in Alazan Apache Courts, located on the west side of San Antonio. Her mother was a seamstress with a ninth grade education and her father, with a fifth grade education, sold ice from his cart. Belle attended J. T. Brackenridge Elementary School, known to barrio residents as "La 21." At the age of seven, Belle started piano lessons, and when she turned ten she and her brother, Roy Jr., began spending their summers in Guadalajara with their maternal grandparents. It was in Guadalajara that she was introduced to mariachi music, and she would return every summer until the age of fifteen to learn about the music.

Belle attended Lanier Middle School and then, in 1947, Lanier High School, where she was student council president and senior class president (just like Leticia). While in high school, Belle helped her parents financially by playing piano in various local bands, such as the Eduardo Martinez International Orchestra and the Felix Solis and Ramiro Cervera Orchestra. She graduated in 1951 and, shortly after, enrolled in Our Lady of the Lake University (at that time an all-girls school) on a scholarship, majoring in music education. She always wanted to teach mariachi music as a tribute to her cultura, and she wanted her students to be proud of their culture.

Leticia's father, Daniel San Miguel Jr., and his twin sister, Delia, were born in San Antonio, Texas, in 1931, at what is now the Baptist Hospital. Delia died 36 hours later. Their father, Daniel San Miguel Sr., was born in 1900 and raised in Eagle Pass, Texas. Daniel Jr.'s mother, Delia Garza Musquiz, was born in 1901 in Mexico and migrated to Texas sometime during the Mexican Revolution. She had a ninth grade education. Daniel San Miguel Jr. was raised about a mile and a half from the drugstore his father owned. He attended St. Agnes Catholic Church for his elementary education, then Horace Mann Junior High School and Thomas Jefferson High School, where he played football and baseball and ran track. In 1948, Daniel entered St. Mary's University (at that time an all-boys school).

Chillona Berrinche

Although Belle and Daniel attended different high schools, from time to time their schools would compete with each other. As he was a jock and she was a cheerleader, they came to know of each other. However, they never socialized or even talked until they were both in college. St. Mary's University had a cheerleading squad comprised of three women from Incarnate Word, a local Catholic women's college, and three from Our Lady of the Lake, one of whom was Belle.

They met and had been dating for nine months when Daniel dropped out of school and entered the U. S. Army. Daniel completed basic training and was given five days' leave. He came back to San Antonio and married Belle on December 12, 1953. He left her with his parents and was then sent off to Fort Chaffee, Arkansas, for leadership training. She soon joined him and they lived for a few months in Fort Smith, Arkansas, about ten miles from Fort Chaffee. From there, the San Miguels would relocate to Fort Lewis, Washington.

Within a year of their relocation, Belle and Daniel were the proud parents of a little girl. She was born in Tacoma, which is a few miles north of Fort Lewis, on December 6, 1954. She weighed 8 pounds 4 ounces and was 19 inches long. Daniel wanted to name his baby girl after his grandmother, Antonia or "Tonita." Belle wanted to name her Rosa, which was short for Rosa Alejandrina, her older sister who passed away at the age of six months. Belle also wanted to name her daughter Leticia. Leticia was the name of a young ladies' social club that Belle knew of when she was growing up. She always liked that name. They finally settled on the name Leticia Rosa.

The San Miguel family came to San Antonio when Leticia was three months old and settled on West Huisache. They were one of very few Hispanic families living in that neighborhood, which was well kept and made up mostly of teachers, attorneys, and local business owners.

As a child, Leticia was nicknamed "Chillona Berrinche" (crying tantrum) because she would push those around her to their limits. She started kindergarten at Mount Sacred Heart and was transferred two years later to Woodland Elementary School. She attended Horace Mann Junior High School until the family moved to Beverly Street, which was four blocks from Thomas Jefferson High School, from where she graduated in 1973. Leticia now lives with her family one block from where she grew up as a child. She has never had the desire to move elsewhere.

Belle went to school while her family was growing. Because of the importance she placed on family, it took her eight years to complete her education degree, which she received in 1969. The first school district Belle worked for was the Edgewood School District; she worked there on an emergency certificate as a music teacher. With the birth of her second child, Daniel III, and subsequent children, Annabelle, Roseanne, and Roland, Belle took some time off work.

Soon afterwards, Belle received a phone call from Joe Leyva, the principal in the North Side School District. Leyva had known Belle when they were at the Edgewood School District and had loved the music she taught her students. He asked if she would teach music at Cable Elementary. The only constraint was that she could not teach any Spanish songs; any other language—German, French, Japanese—was acceptable, just not Spanish. This was before bilingual education had been accepted in the school systems. However, Belle insisted that the school district permit the use of the Spanish language and eventually was able to teach her students songs in Spanish. She was later transferred to Barkley Elementary in the San Antonio School District, where she started the first elementary mariachi group, called *Los Tejanitos.* This is where she learned of the impact music could have on children and the community.

Los Tejanitos evolved out of an after-school program that Belle created to teach children to dance, play guitar, and sing. According to Belle, "It gave the students confidence and feeling of success in what they knew they could do." Belle would take them to perform at the state conventions and Parent Teacher Associations (PTAs). "Having the students perform at PTAs was a great way to get the parents involved in their child's education. Prior to this, parent involvement was lacking."[2] After the success of *Los Tejanitos,* the principal from Lanier High School, Jessie Mendez, asked Belle to start a mariachi program at his school. She was reluctant to accept because she thought teenagers would be embarrassed to wear the traditional *trajes de charro* (suits of charros; horsemen). She was wrong; the mariachi program was a hit. In 1975 she was asked to go to the school's district office and become a specialist in the bilingual programs, where she would oversee the mariachi program for the San Antonio Independent School District.

Belle was the primary breadwinner and the constant parental figure in the San Miguel household. She was very close to her in-laws, and they were very supportive of her and the children. They lived at the Beverly Street house for about ten years. Mary Louis San Miguel, Belle's sister-in-law, lived just one block over on Mulberry Street. Daniel San Miguel Jr. had only one brother, with four kids. Leticia and her siblings always played with their cousins—they were inseparable. Leticia showed leadership skills at a very young age. Belle remembers many instances where Leticia would lead her brothers and sisters from their house to her Aunt Mary Louis for cookies. Even in school she loved to help the teacher and her other classmates.

As a little girl, Leticia was placed by her mother in many extracurricular activities. Leticia was involved with the Girl Scouts, which at the time was one of only a few organizations in San Antonio that accepted blacks, Hispanics, and Jews. Leticia recalls, "The Girl Scouts were a wonderful equalizer because there were organizations when I was growing up where you couldn't join this club or that club, but the Girl Scouts was one where this was your neighborhood and everybody could join."[3] Much like many cities in the South during this period, segregation was enforced. Rodolfo Rosales, in his book *The Illusion of Inclusion,* confirms that the efforts by the white communities in San Antonio, and throughout the Sunbelt region of the United States, were intended to maintain segregation.

As she grew older, Leticia was also placed in dance. Although she tried her best, she thought it was "work." She explains it this way: "I tried. I liked it. I didn't have the discipline. I was way too competitive." However, she thrived in sports. She loved track and football. Since she grew up in an era before Title IX, Leticia and a group of neighborhood kids formed teams. "We didn't have a whole lot of girl sports. In school all you had was volleyball. There was no girls' softball team. There was no girls' track team. There was no girls' swim team." She and the neighborhood kids formed the Woodlawn Lake Runners. Baseball and football teams followed. She loved the competitive nature of football. She played with the neighborhood boys until her father forbade her from playing the game. "When I was 12 or 13 years, my father told me I could no longer play football because I started to grow breasts. I was so angry. I could not understand. And, he just said, 'Because they will tackle you even when you don't have the ball.' I just thought, 'How absurd, what do you mean?' I just had no idea." Leticia would not pick up a football again until she was a pharmacy student at the University of Houston.

After football, at the behest of her mother, Leticia took piano lessons. Since Belle had taken piano lessons, she naturally wanted

Leticia to follow in her footsteps. But Leticia, again, felt it was "work" and thought her time would be better spent in other activities. She convinced her parents to stop spending money on piano lessons and unsuccessfully attempted to persuade them to use the money to convert the family garage into a little a chemistry lab. She wanted to be a pharmacist just like her grandfather—she had known it since the age of six.

Leticia began honing her leadership skills in the ninth grade at Horace Mann Middle School. There, she joined the "White Tide," which was a service organization. She was selected to represent her homeroom, which placed her in student council. During the spring semester of eighth grade, she ran for president of student council to spite her boyfriend. This is how she described the situation:

> My boyfriend at the time, Jaime, was the president of student council. One day I was listening to a conversation between him and some of the other officers in student council. They were all boys. They talked about how it's time to elect officers, like who can they get to run for student council? They were talking about all the names and I was wondering why there weren't any girl's names mentioned for any of the offices, not even secretary. So, they had gone over all the names and finally they had gotten to president. They couldn't really think of anyone so they were going to run Javier, Jaime's little brother. And, I spoke up and said, "I could do it." He looked up and turned around to me and—I will never forget this—he said, "You can't run for student council president." I said, "Why not? Why couldn't I? I am in student council." He said, "'Cause you are a girl." I said (to myself), "wrong thing to say." I said, "I am going to put my name in." So, I went to go and talk to the other girls. Then I went to talk to the other guys that I had grown up with playing sports. And I won. I was my ninth grade student council president at Horace Mann. I would have never thought about it except somebody told me I couldn't because I was a girl. I had

> no idea having a vagina had anything to do with whether or not someone could run for office.

As Leticia was going through junior high in the late 1960s, the women's movement was in its early stages and there was not anything Leticia felt she could not do as a young woman. Her mother's strong maternal influence instilled in her a strong sense of identity and self-confidence.

At Jefferson High School, Leticia excelled. She was a member of the Latin club, the honor society, and she was elected sophomore and junior class president and, in her senior year, president of LASSOS (a pep squad composed of girls who twirled ropes when they marched in halftime shows or parades). LASSOS allowed her to march with the school band and participate in dance routines. She never joined a social club. According to Leticia, "My father had wanted me to be a cheerleader. Back then, there were very few Mexicana cheerleaders and it was not the athletic sport that it is now." But Leticia did not want to be a cheerleader. She said, "I was the person who loved to be the jock. I could not see myself as being someone relegated to someone who cheered for the jock. I just couldn't do it. That was not me."

At Jefferson, Leticia understood the racial tensions surrounding her community. There were only three clubs available: one for white girls, one for Mexican girls, and one for Jewish girls. The racial divides were clearly defined. Her high school did not allow black students until 1968. Until then she never went to school with black students, who had their own high school. As a Mexican, Leticia experienced racism and learned how it could limit future possibilities. Leticia recalls an incident:

> I had taken the SAT my junior year and did really well. I wanted to take it again to improve my score but back then you could not sign up individually for it. Your counselor had to sign you up for it and so I went to my counselor to sign up to take it my senior year and she said, "Oh no, for a Mexican you have great

> scores. You don't need to take it again. Why do you want to go to Princeton? You should be a secretary." I said, "No, I need to take it because I am on the cusp of what would be acceptable for Princeton. I don't want to be a secretary, I want to go to pharmacy school." I mean for a real Ivy League school I was right at the cusp when I took it my junior year. By my senior year I thought, you know, I will do better. Well, I didn't get to up my score because my name was not turned in. I told her I wanted to get into Princeton. And, to her it was like it was out of my realm. I did apply and I did get in but not with the financial aid packet that I needed and could have gotten with a higher score.

Leticia told her mom later about the encounter and her mom said, "*Mi hijita* [my daughter], there isn't anything you can't do if you want to do it. And, if you are getting your scholarship, or they are asking you to go, go." Deep down inside Belle's heart was saying, "Don't go, don't go, don't go!" But, as an educator she was pushing for the best that she could give or do for her children. Leticia was disappointed at what the high school counselor had said. She would not attend Princeton, but she had other plans.

Leticia's second choice was Baylor University. She really wanted to attend Baylor, but her grandmother would not have it. Once she found out that Baylor *ni tenien la Virgen* (doesn't even have the Virgin Mary), her grandmother could not understand how her mother could let *la niña* (the little girl) go to a place that does not have a statue of La Virgen. She said, "*La niña si puede ir a Santa Maria* [the little girl can go to St. Mary's]." Leticia knew that St. Mary's did not have a pharmacy school and that she would eventually have to transfer to a school that did. But, like a dutiful daughter and good granddaughter, Leticia ended up enrolling at St. Mary's University in San Antonio in the fall of 1973. She received the president's scholarship at St. Mary's and used work-study to help pay for school. Leticia always worked. She worked part-time in a biology lab at Brooks Air Force

Base, at San Antonio's Visitor's Bureau, as a guide at the Institute of Texan Cultures, and as a substitute teacher. The latter job was the most difficult job she had ever done.

Leticia's desire to be a pharmacist was instilled by her fraternal grandfather, Daniel San Miguel Sr. He had a pharmacy called the La Botica Guadalupana Drug Store located on Produce Row on the city's near-west side.[4] The building that houses Botica Guadalupana dates back to 1820 and was the first permanent structure on Produce Row. Prior to becoming a drug store in 1893, the building was used as a mercantile dry goods store, a theater-entertainment house with liquor and cockfights, and a house for ladies of questionable character. The first pharmacy on this site was Cowen Drug, which opened in 1893. Juan Leal bought the store in 1912 and changed its name to La Botica Guadalupana.[5] In 1921 Daniel San Miguel Sr. began working for Leal and in 1933 bought the store. Daniel San Miguel Sr. was known as the grandfather of Market Square. Following the death of Daniel Sr. in 1986, the store ceased being a pharmacy by 1987.[6]

Leticia's parents divorced in 1973 when she was a senior in high school. Growing up, Leticia's relationship with her father was somewhat estranged. The San Miguel household was run by the matriarch, Belle. When Leticia entered St. Mary's University, Belle received some financial and emotional help from a family friend, Juan Ortiz. He was one of Belle's former music students at Lanier High School and San Antonio Community College (SACC). She taught one music class at SACC. Belle had helped him receive a scholarship at SACC and a friendship grew. Because of his knowledge of mariachi music, Belle hired him to oversee the mariachi program at the San Antonio Independent School District. Their friendship grew into something more than Belle had expected. He would help Belle with her children by babysitting for them while she dated. He developed a close relationship with the three younger San Miguel children, Annabelle, Roseanne, and Roland. Juan's feelings for Belle evolved much more quickly than Belle's feelings for Juan. Leticia knew of Juan's feeling for her mother early on and advised him not to tell her. Belle had just come out of a divorce and Juan knew it was too early for Belle to enter into another serious relationship. So he patiently waited until Belle was ready. Eight years later, in 1982, they married.

The College Years

During her first year at St. Mary's, Leticia was selected to take part in the Miss Fiesta contest, held every spring in San Antonio. All the local universities select their co-eds at the very beginning of the semester to take part in the contest. At the time, each of the fraternities selected their Miss Fiesta contestants and they would then compete in the Miss Fiesta Pageant sponsored by the City of San Antonio. Participants were judged on speech and poise. There were no bathing suit contests, no talent contest, no cleavage, and you could not wear a dress above the knee. The winner was to act as an ambassador for the City of San Antonio and would receive a $1,000 scholarship, while the first runner-up would receive $750.

Leticia was preparing for biology lab one day in the spring semester of 1974 when she was approached by some of her friends who were members of one of the fraternities. The girl they had selected for the pageant, which was to be held that same day, had become ill and could not participate. They asked Leticia to take her place. Leticia said, "I am not beauty pageant material." Leticia did not see herself as a "foo foo" girl. She did not like wearing makeup. She did not like wearing bows in her hair. She liked playing sports. They said, "Oh yeah, you're pretty. You could do it." Leticia responded, "No." They rebutted, "Do you have a formal?" She said, "No, but I have a formal that I wear to prom." She really was not interested. They pleaded with her. She finally said, "I can't get out of [Brother Donohue's] lab."

They left and went to Brother Donohue, who was head of the biology department, and said, "We need Leticia San Miguel to go down to the City Municipal Auditorium for the Miss Fiesta preliminaries or St. Mary won't be represented." Just as class was about to start, Brother Donohue excused Leticia from lab that day. She went home to ask her mother's permission. She made it through the preliminaries and then went back the next day. Sandra Ojeda from Our Lady of the Lake was selected Miss Fiesta and Leticia was selected as an alternate first runner-up. She ended up carrying out the duties of Miss Fiesta because Sandra had a very restrictive boyfriend and could not do the traveling that was required. Leticia represented San Antonio in a number of other city festivals around Texas. The highlight for Leticia and her family was representing the City of San Antonio at the Tournament of Roses Parade in California.

Enter Mr. Van de Putte

It was Belle that introduced Leticia to her future husband in the spring of 1972. Henry "Pete" Van De Putte Jr. was born in San Antonio on February 21, 1950. Both his parents were born in San Antonio as well. His father, Henry "Pete" Van de Putte Sr., was the owner of the Dixie Flag Manufacturing Company. Pete Jr. received his bachelor of arts in music education from St. Mary's in 1972. Pete was a senior at St. Mary's, doing his student teaching at Lanier High School in the band program while Belle was the choir teacher. Belle would have lunch with Pete and John Rodriguez, the band director, and talk about the music. Each would talk with the others about the band each played in after hours. One day Leticia, then sixteen years of age and a junior in high school, came to pick her mother up from work—her mother never liked to drive—and Mr. Pete Van de Putte, as he was known to her, was talking to her mother outside her classroom. This was the first time that Leticia was introduced to "mom's colleague, Mr. Pete Van de Putte." She thought he was "kinda cute."

A few months after the encounter, she mentioned to her mother that she had broken up with her boyfriend and that he had put out the word around school that no one was to ask her to the junior-senior prom. It was two weeks before the prom and she was the junior class president. After several days of contemplating, Belle mentioned to Pete, "My daughter just broke up with her boyfriend and she doesn't have a date for the junior-senior prom, do you think you could escort her?" When he was asked this, he did not remember that he had met her and said to himself, "Okay, this girl is junior class president and she can't get a date? Man, she must be a dog with a double 'D' because her mother is trying to set her up."[7] He graciously excused himself from the invitation claiming he had a gig that night, which Belle knew that he did not. She never told him the situation. One week later, Leticia came by again to pick her mother up and, again, she was talking with Pete. Pete met Leticia for a second time and realized that this was the daughter that Belle had been talking about. He said to himself, "Idiot, you idiot. What is wrong with you?" Pete was smitten, but Leticia thought of him as nothing more than her mother's colleague. She ended up going to the prom with a friend of her ex-boyfriend.

From then on, she would see Pete occasionally when he would drop sheet music off for Belle at her house. But what actually precipitated them seeing more of each other was when Belle became the director of the Cultural Arts Program in the San Antonio School District in the fall of 1976. She had instituted the mariachi program in the school district. She had mariachis in a couple elementary schools and a couple middle schools, but was unsuccessful at initiating the program in high school. She turned to Pete, who was teaching at Jefferson High School, for help. Pete used his stage band to help her. On Mondays, Wednesdays, and Fridays he would teach them jazz, and on Tuesdays and Thursdays Belle would teach the class mariachi music. Working this close with Belle, Leticia would come to the school to see rehearsals, and this is where she and Pete began to visit.

A year and a half after beginning her studies at St. Mary's, Leticia transferred to the University of Houston to attend pharmacy school. She lived in Bates Dormitory, which was the dormitory where minorities and poor, white, female students lived. The Towers Dormitory was where the sorority girls lived. Although she was segregated, she loved where she lived because they had intramural football. But an injury to her knee during a game ended her playing days. She was not politically active at all except on one issue: housing. She had accompanied her roommate, Maren Thompson, to an on-campus film exhibit. The film documented inequities in housing policies toward gay and lesbian partners. At the time, the City of Houston prohibited two individuals of the same sex from living in one residence. The only student organization addressing this issue was the Young Democrats. But working part-time at a local pharmacy and going to school did not leave her much time to engage in political activity. She participated when time permitted and never really considered herself "political."

Leticia would occasionally return to San Antonio to visit her family. On one such weekend, she was getting ready to go out on a date. She had just finished putting her electric rollers on her hair; she had on panty hose and her robe when she heard someone knocking at the door. She thought it was her brother's friend and opened the front door. It was Pete. She said, "You're not Bob, the little boy that lives down the street." Pete said, "No, I am not." He looked at her kind of funny. At that moment, she realized that she had on her robe with hair curlers. "Excuse me. I am sorry. Is your mom home?" he asked. She said, "No, she is not here." He responded by saying, "I just came by to leave her something," and handed her sheet music. Leticia said, "Okay." And he looked at her with the same odd look in his face and said, "Do you get FM?" He said it with a straight face. She was silent. He repeated it again, "Do you get FM?" She then started laughing, but he never cracked a smile. She said, 'Thanks." He turned around and walked to his car and drove off. As she was closing the door she said, "What a funny man."

By now, Leticia was well into pharmacy school and would come home to visit her family every so often. Every time she did, she would join her mother and several other teachers, Pete included, at various social events after school. Her mother would hear Leticia say, "This guy has a great sense of humor." So her mother set out to set them up.

On one occasion, Leticia met her mother at Jefferson High School. Her mother suggested that Leticia drive with Pete since Leticia was helping him put away the remaining instruments. After they finished, she got into his car and they were ready to drive off when Pete asked, "Where are we going?" And, she said, "Well, I am in your car; wherever we are supposed to go." He said, "Didn't your mother tell you where we are supposed to be?" Leticia responded by saying, "No, she didn't tell you?" "No." This was before cell phones so she could not reach her mother. Leticia finally realized that her mother set them both up. Leticia felt bad and said, "I am sorry. I don't know where we are supposed to go. Just go ahead and take me home." Pete responded by saying, "Hey, you hungry? Do you want to go get a bite?" "Oh, all right," Leticia replied. So they decided to go to a club by the name of The Old Landing to hear Jim Cullen's jazz band and eat. She did not return home until five o'clock the next morning. After that night they would talk for hours on end. After the third date, Leticia questioned whether she should continue to see him and thought, "It's not going to kill me." This went on for about a period of two months. She felt very comfortable talking to him, and she never once grew bored of his company. On the third date, Leticia kissed him good night and remembers shutting the door and saying, "Oh, shit, I am in trouble. I am in trouble." She remembers thinking, "Never did I think anyone would have that effect on me."

They started dating seriously from February to March of 1977. During that time, Pete visited Leticia twice in Houston. In March, Leticia returned home to San Antonio for spring break to spend time with her family and Pete. She and Pete had gotten into a misunderstanding and broke up. She did not talk to him again until June. One Sunday morning in June, Leticia saw Pete five pews in front of her and her family at St. Paul's Catholic Church. It was crowded and he was alone. She heard the priest say, "Peace be with you. Let us share a sign of peace." Leticia left her pew, went up to Pete's, shook his hand and they both said, "Peace be with you." Leticia sat with him until the mass was over. They made plans to meet later that evening and talk over coffee. After returning from church, Pete decided to mow his lawn. While he was mowing the lawn he stopped and decided right then and there to marry Leticia. Later on that Sunday they both talked over coffee and decided they would see each other again.

Pete left for a long vacation to visit his mother in Florida. He returned to San Antonio on July 3 and proposed to her on July 4. She cried and said, "Yes, Pete." Pete had to ask for Belle's permission. Belle responded by saying, "What took you so long Pete?" Belle was delighted; after all, Pete was the one that she picked for Leticia. Belle made Pete promise that Leticia would finish her degree from the University of Houston. She had one year left. He replied, "You don't think I want her to finish? She is going to make me rich." They all laughed. She always thought Pete was the perfect spouse for her daughter but was surprised by the quickness of the engagement.

Pete then had to ask Leticia's father for his blessing. Later that week Pete met Leticia's father for the very first time outside her house. He looked at Pete and said, "Son, you do know what you are getting into?" "Daddy!" Leticia responded. He said, "*Mi hijita* [my daughter], this seems to be a nice young man. He doesn't know you. You are not wife material." He then proceeded to tell Pete, "She is very stubborn, you will never win an argument, she is way too independent, and you will not be the lead person in the family. If you want a wife, she is not a good wife. She is not wife material. I love her but . . ."[8] Leticia knew deep down inside that her father's description of her was right on the money.

Shortly after they began their engagement, Leticia announced that she was going to keep her family's last name of San Miguel. Pete had no objection to that. Leticia's mother, however, disagreed with Leticia and questioned Pete's acquiescence to his soon-to-be wife's decision. Moreover, up until the engagement, Leticia's family called her by her middle name, Rosie. Since she was marrying Pete "Van De Putte" (Belgian descent), she told Pete, in no uncertain terms, that after their marriage she would go by the name of Leticia and that Pete had to pay the rest of her school. If Pete agreed to her terms then she would take his last name. She believed using Leticia rather than Rosie was a constant reminder of her Hispanic heritage. They had joked about hyphenating her name to be Leticia Rosa San Miguel-Van De Putte but they figured her name would really be too long.

Leticia never imagined herself as a wife, let alone a mother. She had a list of things she wanted to do before she got married and settled down. She wanted to become a pharmacist and own her own business. She wanted to drive an expensive red sports car and buy her mother a washer and dryer. Instead she and Pete developed a plan, which was for her to finish pharmacy school and marry in June or July of 1978.

Leticia returned to school in late-August 1977. She fell in her bathroom one day and suffered a terrible concussion. She was taken to the Houston hospital and eventually transferred to a hospital in San Antonio. She had lost her ability to read and to stand for very long periods and even lost control of her own bowel movements for ten days. When she returned to school two weeks later, she had fallen so far behind that it was impossible for her to catch up. She went to the dean and asked for a medical withdrawal.

She now had to decide whether to stay in Houston and work or return to San Antonio, live at home and work until the following year, when she could enter a new rotation cycle. Pete said, "Let's just get married now." If Leticia was going to get married before she returned to school, she would have to decide whether to return to Houston or commute from San Antonio to Austin. She decided to transfer to the College of Pharmacy at the University of Texas at Austin. Leticia and her mother had six weeks to plan the wedding. Leticia and Pete married on October 23 at St. Paul's Catholic Church and had seven hundred people at the reception, which was held at San Antonio Homebuilders Hall. She entered her final year of pharmacy school in the fall of 1978 and graduated cum laude in the spring of 1979. Pete ended his teaching career as band director at Jefferson High School in 1980 and became CEO of the family business.

Politics y La Communidad

Leticia's first job out of college was a pharmacist consultant with T. L. Vorden Baumen and Associates in San Antonio. A clinical rotation at San Antonio's State Hospital had made her an attractive recruit. She worked there from 1980 to 1982, then at her grandfather's pharmacy at the Guadalupana for about two and a half years. Her grandfather's pharmacy also sold herbal medicines. This put her in contact with a number of local *curanderos*[9] and she was exposed to this "underground medical system."

While working at her grandfather's pharmacy, she learned about people, the needs of the community, and its problems. One of the problems she had to deal with as a small business owner in the Market Square was urination. Every morning when Leticia arrived to open up the Guadalupana, the front door always smelled of urine. Every morning she ended up hosing the urine off the front door. She complained to city council and was placed by the mayor at the time, Henry Cisneros, on the advisory board, Centro 21. Cisneros created Centro 21 to help revitalize downtown. As a member of Centro 21, Leticia's first political issue was "potty parity" for downtown. She argued that even though San Antonio encouraged people to have a good time drinking and eating, the city provided no public restrooms, which tourists and shoppers constantly complained about.[10] When the tourists had to use the restroom, they were left with two options: either walk all the way back to their hotel or relieve themselves in public. Leticia found that it was easier for people to choose the latter of the two options. She unsuccessfully tried to get the city to build more restrooms.

Leticia's political activity at the grassroots level was expanding. When she saw something wrong in her community, she complained and was placed on a board. She never considered her actions political. To her, she was doing what she could for the betterment of her community. For example, in the 1980s she was placed on the Airport Advisory Board. Her grandmother, Memo, had had a stroke and was confined to a wheelchair. She subsequently had an accident in a bathroom at San Antonio Airport because the airport was not in compliance with the Americans with Disabilities Act. Leticia complained. "You know what government does at any level when you complain, and particularly when you get your data and research behind you and go to city council or commissioner's court? They put you on a damn committee," she says.

After leaving her grandfather's pharmacy, she worked part-time at Loma Park Pharmacy, located on Culebra Street in San Antonio's west side. The clientele was predominately Latino and poor. Within a couple years, Leticia bought the store and became the owner. Then, in 1987, she expanded her business to include herbal medicines, just like her grandfather's pharmacy. With a new business and young children at home, Leticia did not have time for anything else in her life. But the west side of San Antonio had problems that Leticia could not ignore. Flooding was (and still is) a significant problem in San Antonio, especially around some of the parks. Leticia noticed that parks on the north side of town, like McAllister and Raymond Russell, received renovations to deal with flooding, but Rodriguez Park, near her pharmacy on the west side, was in disrepair. She joined forces with the Edgewood Business Community and local area churches and together they went to Commissioners Court to demand that their park receive the same attention as the other two parks. Not long after that, she was placed on the park's advisory board.

Most of Leticia's political experience at this point in her life was at the grassroots level and as a campaign volunteer. When she was growing up, the front yard of the San Miguel household always had a political sign supporting her godfather Joel Bernal's run for state representative and, later, state senate. On election days, she worked the poll sites. After she married Pete, she continued to play a supportive role in campaigns. Pete first became involved in politics when his colleague at Jefferson High School, Paul Elizondo decided to run for state representative in 1978. Pete became his campaign treasurer, while Leticia was behind the scenes, walking blocks, stuffing envelopes, hosting tea parties, and helping wherever she was needed. She was also always pregnant. As Elizondo recalls, "My first election was the only time Leticia was not pregnant. Every time I ran for office after that, she was always pregnant. But, she was always out there campaigning for me block walking."[11] She had six children in nine years of marriage.[12] She was famous for taking her six children block walking with her during campaigns.

In his book, *The Illusion of Inclusion*, political scientist Rodolfo Rosales writes about Mexican American political participation in San Antonio politics in the post–World War II era. In it, he discusses the role of Mexican American women in the electoral and party politics of San Antonio. He contends that they rarely played a leadership role beyond the precinct, nor did they run for office, nor officially run a campaign; they were there, but in a supportive role. According to Rosales, Mexican American women were, for all practical purposes, invisible, especially when it came to the media of the day. To this day, the patriarchal system in the political process, after all was said and done, is still safe and sound.[13]

As far back as 1968, when political scientist Edwin Dickens observed, "Most, if not all, Mexican American women were not encouraged to participate in politics," lack of formal education, occupational segregation, marriage, and motherhood prevented women's political participation. Few graduated from high school. Only a small percentage of women were employed outside the home and most working women were not in occupations that made them part of an independent middle class. There were no Mexican American female lawyers. Working women had less control over their labor time: clerks, for instance, could not take time off from their workplace as easily as male business owners.[14] But, they participated directly in Democratic Party precinct politics, where the political mobilization of voters took place. In terms of leadership at this more informal grassroots level, Chicanas were quite active and quite visible.

As her children entered school, Leticia's participation expanded. She was involved in the PTA at her children's school, St. Joseph's Catholic Church, Bexar County Pharmacy Association, and the Mexican American Business and Professional Women's Club (MABPW), and was a city council appointee to the Mayor's Commission on the Status of Women. MABPW was perhaps the most political of all the organizations Leticia joined. It was created in 1972 by Maria Antonietta Berriozábal, and several other Chicanas in an effort to elevate the image of the Mexican American woman in the community. The organization was immediately immersed in electoral politics as it supported political candidates who were sensitive to the needs of Chicanas. Through MABPW, these women were able to address the problems of isolation and neglect that Chicanas found not only in the business world, but also in the professional world.

Little did she know that all her memberships would translate into a political network that would prove to be her base of support for elected office. It was only a matter of time before she decided to run for political office, though she expressed no ambition for it early on. For now, she was happy being, what Rosales calls a, "soldier in the political trenches."[15] She was, like many of the Chicanas at the time, intimately involved in the organizing and mobilizing that formed the backbone of the coalition's precinct strategy.

Summary

As we see in this chapter, the cultural expectations espoused by her grandmother limited Leticia's independence, initially. She was able to eventually break away from these constraints through education, which opened up a whole new world of possibilities for her. Prior to her marriage, her involvement in politics was superficial, that is, working at poll sites for her *compadre* Joe Bernal and displaying political signs in the front yard. She was too busy with school to fully engage in politics. Her marriage to Pete and his involvement in politics got her involved in politics. At first it was only at the supportive level. But as she matured and her family expanded, so did the level of her political involvement.

When there was an issue that the community needed resolved, she did not seek personal favors from her representatives, as is what normally occurs in local politics. To do this would mean that the constituent "owes" a favor to the representative from whom assistance was sought. Instead, she took it upon herself to resolve the complaint. This way she was not beholden to any party officials or representatives. She complained, led the charge for change and, in return, she was placed on numerous boards. An interesting point of analysis is that Leticia never viewed her complaining to city council as a political activity. To her it was just addressing a problem that affected her community. This is consistent with the literature on women in politics. Women tend not to see anything political with their involvement on boards, but it is here where they are informally trained to take leadership positions in the community as well as build a base of support. As her community activism grew, so did her professional activism. Unbeknownst to her, the political and professional activity she engaged in, that is, organizing various sectors within the community, gave her experience and confidence.

FOUR

Making Connections Between Politics and Community

THE LAST CHAPTER focused on Van de Putte's early years and her political socialization. This chapter focuses on Van de Putte's initiation into electoral politics and her years as a state representative. Until she attempted to move from the House to the Senate, she never really had a serious challenger during all her years in office. Van de Putte's rise to the top was not by any means easy or traditional. San Antonio's political environment was no more inviting than the state's political environment for Mexican American women. The goal of this chapter is to understand how both environments served as obstacles to participation in electoral politics by Latina women.

A Word About Mexican American Women in San Antonio Politics

Before 1968, Mexican American women served as campaign managers, campaign workers, fund raisers, contributors, voters, and precinct chairs, but records of their participation were not kept. In Texas, women in the Raza Unida Party (RUP) made major contributions to the organization and increased their own empowerment. In 1977, single-member districting allowed more Mexican Americans to win offices and allowed Mexican American women to gain office for the first time. The feminist movement and the Chicano movement, which dated back to 1965, made this possible.[1] Participation in the RUP and the Citizens Organization for Public Service provided leadership training for women.

Thus the 1970s witnessed the start of Mexican American women attaining highly visible political roles. Olivia Garza was appointed to fill her husband's post on the city council. RUP candidate Irma Mireles won a seat on the San Antonio River Authority Board in 1977, unseating incumbent William Hayman, and Yolanda Torres ran for a seat on the Texas Board of Education. In 1981, Maria Antonietta Berriozábal was the first Mexican American woman and one of four Mexican Americans elected to city council (a position she held for ten years); she was followed by Yolanda Vera in 1985.[2] In 1991, Berriozábal was the first Chicana to run for mayor. Van de Putte's coming of age was at a turning point for Latinas in San Antonio's political scene.

It was not until the 1990s when Leticia Van de Putte's political career really began. By this time, the Van de Putte family had begun a direct marketing herbal business called Aloe Vera, which was run out of a building adjoined to the Loma Park pharmacy. They had also just purchased a bigger house and were raising six children. In March of 1990 the state primaries were held. State Representative Orlando Garcia of District 115 ran unopposed and was on his way to the general election in November. A few months after the primaries, a seat on the Fourth District Court of Appeals became vacant. The county precinct chairs of the court met and selected Orlando Garcia to run for the seat. In August, Orlando resigned his place on the ballot for state representative in order to run for the appeals court, and his representative seat became vacant. If a seat becomes vacant after the primary, Texas's electoral rules dictate that a special candidate selection procedure must follow. Because primaries are a function of the parties, party officials (precinct chairs) select the nominee to fill the vacant seat. Van de Putte was one of the twenty precinct chairs in District 115.

Van de Putte had been a precinct chair since 1988. Consistent with the literature on women in politics, she was *asked* (not recruited) to fill this post by a party representative, or, in this case, her state representative, Orlando Garcia. In San Antonio's Democratic Party politics, serving as a precinct chair was the highest level of participation a Latina could experience. Even then, party politics was one of alienation because of its top-to-bottom organization.[3] She recalls how she became precinct chair: "I received a call at my store from State Representative Orlando Garcia about a vacant precinct chair. He was frantic and said, 'We don't have anybody running the precinct . . . there is nobody filing in your precinct.' I said, 'What about Mr. so and so?' He said, 'He is not going to.' 'Well what do I need to do?' 'No, no, no, it is just a precinct chair; you won't have to do anything. You will just go to a meeting maybe quarterly . . . ' I said, 'Oh, okay.' So he came over with the paperwork so that I could sign up to be a precinct chair. So it was not that I got recruited; he asked me and there was a vacancy and he didn't want there to be a vacancy." It was to Representative Garcia's advantage to ask somebody he knew to fill the vacancy. Political loyalty in San Antonio can go a long way when it is cashed in at the right time, and it is also just good politics to have someone you know in a party position.

When Garcia's seat became vacant after the primaries, it was up to the party to find a replacement to run on the November ballot. The twenty precinct chairs held a closed meeting to select the new candidate. The five candidates chosen were all male: Steven Sinkin, Robbie Vasquez, Charlie Jones, Bob Cuomo, and David Garcia (the son of the former state representative Matt Garcia). Each had thirty days to convince the precinct chairs that he was the best candidate to replace Orlando Garcia. One day, when Van de Putte had just gotten off the phone with one of the candidates, she mentioned to her husband, Pete, that "all of these guys are nice but not one of them is talking about issues that are important to me." Pete said, "Like what?" She replied, "Well, none of them are talking about children's issues, none of them are talking about small business issues, none of them are talking about health care . . ." Pete interrupted and said, "Well, you run." "I couldn't win." He replied, "Well, of course not, it's too late. But if you only have twenty people voting, if you can get two or three with you, that's enough for you to find out who is going to win and kind of leverage that and get them to support your issues. That is how politics works." She said, "Oh, okay." They both sat down and composed her portfolio on their home computer, took a quick photograph of the family, and generated a candidate profile pamphlet. They spent about 56 dollars. They mailed the pamphlets out to the other twenty precinct chairs and she started to call people.

The Van de Puttes figured that about half of the twenty precinct chairs had actually committed their support to one of the five candidates. By this time there were two front-runners: Steven Sink, a local attorney, and Robbie Vasquez, Garcia's administrative assistant. Van de Putte phoned the other precinct chairs and said, "I understand if you have already committed your first vote to someone else. If by any chance they are out of it, could I have your second vote?" Every one of those twenty people said, "Well, yeah." When the day of the vote came, Leticia Van de Putte was almost nobody's first choice, but she was everybody's second choice. No one thought she could win.

The Van de Puttes began to strategize. Pete went to Bill Marriman, who was one of the precinct chairs, and asked Bill to nominate Leticia. Bill asked Pete if she had any support among the twenty precinct chairs and Pete lied by saying, "Yes." Marriman agreed only if Pete would write the nominating speech; Pete went home and wrote one. This meant that Marriman's vote was now committed to Leticia. Going into the election, she had two votes: her own and Marriman's. The Van de Puttes and Marriman knew that the very first vote was the most crucial one because it was the procedural vote. The Van de Puttes knew that Steven and Robbie had ten votes between them. There were two ways to proceed: top down or bottom up. Top down meant that the top two vote-getters would be placed in a runoff to determine the nominee. Bottom up, also called the "totem pole" method, meant that after a vote was held the lowest vote-getter would be eliminated. This process would be continued until one person was left. The totem pole procedure was Van de Putte's best bet. Bill Marriman cast the first vote and made a motion to go from the bottom up. When the first vote was taken, Van de Putte had three votes, and it snowballed from there. Everybody's first choice kept getting knocked off and their second vote went to Van de Putte. She ended up winning her party's nomination for District 115.

Neither Leticia nor her husband ever thought it was possible for her to win. They got into their car and looked at each other and said, "Now what the hell do we do?" It was an exciting time because she and Christine Hernandez, who had just been elected to District 124 in the primary, were going to be the two new Latina state representatives from Bexar County. Moreover, there were very few people in the legislature passionate about health care, and certainly very few legislators, male or female, with six children. Thus, she was a candidate with a different profile. She was not beholden to anybody's political machine, she was not the favorite of the Democratic Party, and she was not the favorite of unions or trial lawyers. She was viewed as a nice lady and a good little campaign worker.

The Van de Puttes went home to tell their children that their mom was going to run for state representative. Their seven-year-old son, Henry, asked, "Why does mommy need to run for state representative?" Nicole, then ten years old, responded, "Because there are not enough mommies there." Of the 150 members of the House of Representatives, only eight were women. Leticia later said, "From the mouth of a babe; there weren't enough women there."

Enter Bart Simpson

Leticia Van de Putte was now on the ballot for the Democratic Party, and she had no Republican challenger because no one had originally challenged Orlando Garcia. Then Secretary of State George Bayoud Jr. stepped in and announced that the Republican Party could nominate someone because the Democrats nominated someone new. A new opponent arose, 24-year-old Barton "Bart" Simpson, although he posed no serious competition. He worked for a firm that provided interim financing for construction projects, and he often used the pop cultural icon of Bart Simpson at many of his campaign events.[4]

On October 21, 1990, KLRN Public Television Channel 9 in San Antonio sponsored a "Polithon '90" for the November 6, 1990, elections. The candidates had one thirty-minute debate. Leticia Van de Putte, thirty-five years of age, had two challengers: David Galbraith, the Libertarian, who presented no real electoral threat, and Bart Simpson, the Republican challenger. Van de Putte was dressed in a conservative dark suit with a white collar and white pearls, and she was politically conscious of her surroundings. She understood the power of the media. Unlike the other two candidates, when she spoke she looked directly into the camera. At the beginning of the debate, Van de Putte identified three issues that she would focus on if elected: education, health, and issues pertaining to small businesses. She was consistent with Little, Dunn, and Deen's study on gender differences in legislative priorities among state legislative leaders. They found that women leaders are more likely to report issues of traditional concerns to women as priorities: health care, social services, family, children's issues, and the environment.[5] Simpson identified his two issues as being education and crime. Galbraith identified his main issue as working to limit big government.

Van de Putte slowly took command of the debate. As the thirty-minute televised debate came to a close, each candidate made a closing statement. Galbraith spoke first, followed by Simpson. Here, Simpson made a crucial mistake. Rather than neutralizing the gender factor between Van de Putte and himself, he emphasized it in an attempt to mobilize the voters into believing that he would make a better representative. His closing remarks were as follows: "I have the time and energy to represent you in Austin. To work for good education for our children. To help fight crime by keeping young people in school and off the streets. I don't understand how my opponent, with six young children and a business, can feel like she has the time and energy to effectively carry our voice and needs in Austin. I can travel that road for you. Being a representative should not be a part-time job. It is and should be a full-time position. My commitment to the people of District 115 is to be an effective voice and a listening ear in Austin. I ask for your vote on November 6th."[6] Van de Putte picked up on the gender comment and responded by saying, "While it is true that I do have six small children it is because of those very six children that

I feel compelled to do the best job in Austin. I am asking for my family to support me and they have. My children are the driving force, and not only my children but the children of every working family. I don't understand how you can say that as a woman I can't do that job because you are almost condemning every working woman who has to bring home a paycheck and also be a mother. But not just women, every single parent. Men and women are both parents and I feel like I can represent the working families the best. I would be honored to be your state representative."[7] As reported in Garcia and others' study on the first Latina elected officials in the state of Texas, Latinas often faced questions about their ability to represent constituents while fulfilling their expected gender roles as mothers, wives, and grandmothers.[8] Simpson's remark about Van de Putte's motherly duties struck a chord with voters. Some of her constituents would ask her, "While you are in office, who is going to take care of your kids?" She would respond by saying, "My children . . . my husband." Her constituents would reply in a surprising tone, "Your husband is going to babysit your kids?" "No, my husband is going to parent our children. If I don't babysit my own children why would my husband babysit his own children? It is called parenting." She received these kinds of questions from older, mostly Hispanic, men and women.

In San Antonio, during every election cycle, the *San Antonio Express News* invites candidates who want to represent San Antonio at every level of electoral office for an interview and a review of their positions and backgrounds. The newspaper then publishes its list of recommended candidates to voters. This election cycle was particularly exciting for Chicanas running for elected office, because San Antonio had three Chicanas vying for elected office: Maria Antonietta Berriozábal, the first Chicana to run for a mayoral seat in a major U.S. city; Christine Hernandez; and Leticia Van de Putte. The leadership ability of these three Chicanas was never a question. The only question raised was targeted at Berriozábal's "sophistication in matters of economic development."[9] The *San Antonio Express News* endorsed Christine Hernandez for District 124 and Van de Putte for the office of State Senate District 115 by saying, "[She] is a serious candidate with well thought-out views on economic development, education and the environment. She will bring a needed mother's perspective to the Legislature."[10] However, the *Express News* did not endorse Berriozábal's candidacy, and on November 6, Berriozábal garnered 47 percent of the vote but lost to Nelson Wolff.[11] Hernandez won with 100 percent of the vote and Van de Putte won the election with 71.63 percent of the vote (Simpson and Galbraith garnered 24.76 percent and 3.65 percent, respectively).

Van de Putte was off to the House of Representatives. She attributed her victory "to family efforts in daily door-to-door campaigning in her district." "Even the little one went with us," she said. "It was a family thing."[12] In 1990, Rosales assessed the political status of Mexican American women, noting, "Chicano women are significant political actors in San Antonio's electoral politics."[13]

Within a month of her election, Van de Putte's first official act was to participate in the Bexar County Delegation to the Legislature that told the city council that state members were concerned about possible overruns in building the Alamodome and warned they would not support any future requests to "bail out the city of San Antonio on this project." The $177 million Alamodome project was being financed through the levy of a half-cent sales tax by VIA Metropolitan Transit, which was authorized to do so by the legislature in May 1987. Van de Putte noted that the local delegation prevailed in the waning hours of a special session to win authorization for the sales tax, subject to approval by local voters, who approved the levy in a referendum in January 1989.[14]

Learning the "Good Ol' Boy" System

For freshmen state legislators like Van de Putte, legislative orientation took place in December, approximately one month before the session got underway. The *San Antonio Express News* defined the Texas Legislature's Seventy-second Regular Session as one plagued by "mega problems."[15] One of these problems was that the 1991 members would need anywhere from $3.5 billion to $4.5 billion in additional revenue to maintain the current levels of services during the next two fiscal years. In addition, just about everyone agreed that the Texas Supreme Court would find that the school funding plan did not meet constitutional requirements and that the legislature would have to try again to deal with school funding. Meanwhile, despite heavy investment in new prisons, county jails were forced to house thousands of state prisoners, and the shortage of prison beds forced the early release of thousands more. There was also a strong indication that the U.S. Supreme Court would soon overhaul the way Texas selected its judges so that minorities would have a fair chance to be chosen. Finally, legislators were facing the chores of redistricting, or reapportioning congressional and legislative districts, to match the results of the 1990 census.[16] School funding and redistricting are two issues that define Texas politics, and the latter would propel Van de Putte into the national political arena.

The Seventy-second Legislature was heavily dominated by men. Van de Putte quickly learned that knowing the issues and working toward a solution were not enough, and that the legislature was a representative democracy. She learned that she had a constituency not only in San Antonio, but in Austin as well; 149 representatives in the House, thirty-one senators, and the lieutenant governor and governor would have to depend on her, from time to time, for help with issues of concern to them. Furthermore, she depended on them, as well. If she was going to take on an issue, she was going to need help. "Government is massive," she said. "It is about K through 12 and higher education. It is about the prison system and all the laws. It is about juvenile probation. It is about environmental quality. It is about electricity. It is about utilities. It is about oil and gas. It is about insurance. It is about banking—huge areas, and you cannot know them all, so you have to make the relationships."[17] The first year she spent building relationships, forging coalitions, and learning.

During her first term, Glen Maxey, a Democrat from Austin, was in a special election runoff for a seat in the Texas legislature. Maxey was openly gay. A group of male House colleagues approached Van de Putte because they knew Maxey was in a runoff with a Hispanic candidate. In a strong Texan drawl they said, "Leticia, is there any way we can help that Hispanic in the Austin race? We don't want a homosexual on this House floor." She replied, "Well, I think it is up to the good people of Austin to decide who they want to elect. I am very happy to hear that you want to increase the Hispanic representation in the legislature, but I think the people of Austin . . ." "You mean you don't care if there is a homosexual in this chamber?" Van de Putte replied, "No, I don't. It is not going to bother me. It's not going to bother the men and women, but it might bother the little girls and boys in this chamber." "You mean you wouldn't mind if there were to be a goddamned homosexual on this House floor?" Finally, she realized that she was not getting anywhere by trying to calm their fears. "Hell no," she told them, "he is going to be pissing in your bathroom, not mine." They started laughing. They realized how ridiculous their comments were and decided against involving themselves in Maxey's race. Glen Maxey won the election, but Van de Putte knew there were still a lot of worried folks in the House.

In keeping with tradition, the Speaker of the House, then Gib Lewis, formally welcomed each new member. When Maxey arrived, the Speaker announced his presence, "We welcome newly elected State Representative Glen Maxey to the legislature." People were clapping politely, and Van de Putte got up from her desk, walked to where he was standing. She said, "Hi. Kiss me on the lips." He looked at her, a bit puzzled. She repeated, "I said kiss me!" She gave him a kiss right on the lips and said, "Hi sweetie, I am Leticia. Let me show you where you are sitting." He was surprised but went along with Van de Putte. Later that day he asked her, "What were you doing?" She replied, "These guys are so worried about you being gay and AIDS and HIV, and I thought if I gave you a big smack on the lips and I am a pharmacist and I am Hispanic with six kids that they would realize how stupid their fears are." Maxey knew he had some challenges to face during his first term. The other representatives thought he was going to be a single-issue legislator (focused on homosexual issues), but he was not. He eventually earned the respect of his colleagues.

Van de Putte was somewhat of a maverick on the House floor: she did things her way. For example, it is customary for the Speaker of the House to recognize female colleagues as "Ms.," whether or not they are married. Upon learning this, Van de Putte requested that she be recognized as "Mrs." rather than "Ms." because she was married. Her female colleagues questioned why she would challenge the tradition of the House floor and tried unsuccessfully to convince her accept the traditional title of "Ms."

Towards the end of her first term, Van de Putte decided to sell her pharmacy so that she could remain in the legislature and avoid a possible conflict of interest. She was a member of the Committee on Human Services, which oversees legislation regulating drug vendor contracts for the Texas Department of Human Services, the state's chief welfare agency. Medicaid, which contracts with the Department of Human Services to provide low-cost medical supplies and services for low-income families,[18] constituted approximately 60 to 80 percent of her clientele. She said, "I did something very strange. I read the [state] constitution when I got elected because I figured I swore on it I might as well read it and I myself asked the question, . . . 'Am I in conflict of interest because I vote for the budget that pays for the Medicaid program that sets the reimbursement rates?'" The attorney general at the time, Dan Morales, reported that Van de Putte had to sell her business or resign from the state legislature, based on the conflict of interest argument. The federal government stepped in and said there was no conflict of interest and that she did not need to sell her business. A few years later, in 1994, she sold her business anyway to avoid any perception of conflict of interest.

Van de Putte believed that her profession provided her with some level of acceptance and advantage when it came to issues of health care. She was always prepared for committees, knew what bills were coming up, and was inquisitive, because she was not part of the good ol' boy network. She participated in none of the networking that occurred on the golf course, on hunting trips, or at country western dancing events. She became known as somebody on the floor who could help influence votes on health care and other important issues. On one occasion, the House was about to break for lunch and a colleague, Mark Stiles, a Democrat from Beaumont and chairman of the Calendars Committee, approached her about a particular bill. He said in his Texan drawl, "Van de Putte, we are going to make a motion to reconsider as soon as we get back from lunch. I need you to turn five people from this list from 'no' votes to 'yes' votes." And she said, "This bill?" Stiles responded, "Yep." It was a bill that they had just defeated, and it was not her bill. He continued, "We are coming back in an hour and a half; see what you can do." She said, "Okay." She looked at the list, went to her office to learn as much as she could about the bill, and attempted to track down some members. When the House reconvened, Stiles asked, "Well, what do you got?" She replied, "I got three to turn and two who are going to find legs."[19] The bill passed.

On each of the next three days, Van de Putte found that she had two bills scheduled for debate, which is very unusual in the Texas state legislature, especially for a freshman legislator. The Calendar Committee members challenged Chairman Stiles, asking, "How come you keep doing Van de Putte bills and Van de Putte bills? All of a sudden she gets her bills on the calendar." Stiles replied, "Her ass turned five votes and when your ass can turn five votes then you get two bills a day." Shortly thereafter, the Speaker of the House placed her on the Conference Committee, even though she had no knowledge about the bill. She approached him and said, "I appreciate you putting me on the Conference Committee but this is major stuff that I know nothing about." He replied, "I just need you to keep the boys in the room and keep them talking." She became known as someone who could work the process and find a compromise.

Should She or Shouldn't She?

After Van de Putte's first term as state representative, Republican senator Cindy Krier vacated her state senatorial seat. A state Senate redistricting plan had been formally unveiled, sending a clear signal about her political future. Under the new redistricting plan, Krier's

Senate District 26 would become a Hispanic-majority (61 percent) Democratic district that would stretch from the center of Bexar County all the way to El Paso. Under the original plan, Krier's district included a chunk of north Bexar County and stretched through Guadalupe, Comal, Kendall, Burnet, and Bell Counties. The district, which was 74 percent Anglo, included part of Travis and Williamson Counties.[20] Political observers had closely watched Lieutenant Governor Bob Bullock's negative treatment of Krier since he took office in January 1991. The new redistricting plan was reportedly crafted with Bullock's oversight. Bullock bumped Krier from the Senate Finance Committee and then removed her from a worker's compensation panel in a very repugnant public fashion.[21] This treatment was payback: prior to the 1990 election she had backed Bullock's Republican opponent, and Bullock never forgot. Thus with Bullock as lieutenant governor, Krier knew that she had reached the end of her political career. She was placed on committees that did not really help her district, her bills were never called to the floor, and she was essentially ignored. The city of San Antonio knew that they could not go to her for help with any city issue because her viability as a legislator was nonexistent. As soon as her term was up, she ran and was elected as county judge for the city of San Antonio.

Krier's departure presented Van de Putte with an opportunity. Rumors surfaced in April of 1991 that Van de Putte, among other colleagues, was a potential candidate for the Democratic nomination for Krier's Senate seat.[22] Gregory Luna, a Van de Putte family friend, was a state representative who was also thinking of running for Krier's seat. Luna came from a very large family in San Antonio. County Commissioner Paul Elizondo, her *compadre* (godfather), told Van de Putte, "There are a lot more of his family than San Miguels or Van de Puttes, especially. Not only that, but you are taking on an icon." She may have very well been able to win but, as Elizondo remembers saying, "the females in his family would come after [her]." He advised Van de Putte to stay where she was. Her husband was offended and thought that Elizondo had been influenced by Leo Alvarado, another member of the House of Representatives who desired the state Senate seat as well.[23] Elizondo argued that if you challenge Luna and lose, "your goose is cooked." The base of support for Van de Putte was the same as that for Luna and Elizondo, and in San Antonio there were a number of people that liked Luna. The rule of thumb in San Antonio politics is that you wait your turn. Such an unwritten policy shows respect, and with this comes political support. "Respect in politics in San Antonio is important to our people," said Elizondo. He believed that, "By not running, she solidified her base of support and she showed respect, therefore she got a lot of respect."

In January of 1992, Van de Putte had a health scare that convinced her not to run. A year earlier she had health problems and had seen her gynecologist several times. He recommended that she have a hysterectomy, but she kept putting it off because she was always in a special session. In the latter part of 1991, the governor called four special sessions that carried over into 1992. In January of 1992, she was in a special session in the House chambers and she started to bleed. She was rushed to the hospital and four hours later had an emergency hysterectomy. This incident convinced her not to run for the Senate seat. There would be no way that she could blockwalk or campaign in time for the March 1 primaries. Her critics said, "She made a personal decision that will avoid a political bloodbath between her and state Representative Gregory Luna."[24]

It's Always about the Issues

During the 1992 election season, Van de Putte, age thirty-seven, was one of five Democrats to run unopposed in the March 10 primary elections. In April she discovered that only Libertarian David Galbraith would challenge her in the November elections. Her politically weak opponent ensured her return as a sophomore to the Texas House of Representatives in 1993 for two reasons.[25] First, she had faced him before when she was first elected and beaten him hands down. Second, in Texas, independent candidates running at the state level almost never win.

Among the issues facing Bexar County's contested races were drug-free school zones, education reform, the economy, and tax cuts. Van de Putte's platform was to co-sponsor legislation for weapon-free and drug-free school zones and expand preschool children's immunization programs. She also supported a trust fund for children's nutrition to insure that youngsters starting school were properly nourished.[26] Galbraith, thirty-nine years old, owner of the Newborn Bathtub Refinishing Co., ran on a platform that protested excessive taxation and promoted putting health-care decisions back in the hands of individuals rather than the government.[27]

Shortly after the primary elections, the *San Antonio Express News* gave Van de Putte a subtle endorsement by awarding her the 1992 *Express News* Outstanding Women in Arts award. This award is given to women who display leadership qualities in their respective fields of endeavor.[28] Shortly thereafter, Van de Putte was one of eleven women honored by the Mujeres Project for their work in AIDS services. This organization runs a nonprofit program to prevent sexually transmitted diseases, particularly AIDS, among Hispanic women.[29] One month later, Van de Putte accepted an appointment to the advisory board of Southwestern Capital Markets Inc., an investment banking firm.[30] She won another endorsement by the Bexar County Federation of Teachers for her work on education issues in the 1991 legislature.[31] To gain this endorsement, lawmakers were assessed on their support of teacher career ladder stipends, funds for kindergarten and vocational education programs, and waivers to the twenty-two-pupil limit on class size. Teachers also looked favorably on lawmakers who supported the major school finance reform bill, along with appropriations and tax legislation that accompanied it.[32] Finally, less then a month before voters went to the polls, a conservative group known as the Texans for Governmental Integrity published a voter's guide for Bexar County residents. They endorsed Van de Putte over her Libertarian challenger David Galbraith.[33]

One of the biggest issues of her second term was the fight by doctors from Santa Rosa and Methodist Hospitals and various community interest groups to build a "megahospital" on the northwest side of San Antonio. Critics of the tentative proposal wanted to build the hospital somewhere near the South Texas Medical Center, arguing that a new facility located there could best serve all segments of the community, including low-income patients. Backers of this downtown location were concerned that the megahospital would cause Santa Rosa Children's Hospital to wither, despite promises that children's services would be maintained downtown. Doctors from Santa Rosa and Methodist Hospitals envisioned two children's hubs, one downtown and one to the northwest. The concern was that many low-income patients would be unable to reach the northwest hospital. Van de Putte's position was clear: "A northwest site would be unfair to the southern sector, home to a large number of poor and minorities. We're going to lose, public health-wise, a whole generation of children. It doesn't make sense."[34] She told the proponents of the northwest hospital that she had asked the Texas Department of Health, which licenses new hospitals, to hold a public hearing on the location, acknowledging that the department has no authority to dictate the hospital's location.

On November 3, 1992, Van de Putte was reelected with 85 percent of the vote. Seven days after the election, Governor Ann Richards called a special session to deal with public school funding. Earlier that year, the Texas Supreme Court declared that the legislature's last attempt at reforming public school finance was unconstitutional, but delayed its ruling until June 1 of 1993 to give lawmakers another chance to craft a valid funding plan.[35] This was perhaps a strategic move on the governor's part. Thirty-four members of the 150-member House and eight of thirty-one senators would not return to Austin in January when the Seventy-third Legislature convened. Most of those outgoing legislators had faced the thorny issues of school financing before. Now, however, they could do so without the fear of political reprisal. The legislators were "a little more fiercely independent than if you have the continuing responsibility of facing the electorate again," said John Traeger, a former state senator and representative from Seguin. He also said that, "Those in charge are fearful of what they might do because they're independent [and] a new bill is more apt to be passed."[36] This special session marked the third attempt by the legislature to revamp the school funding system since the Texas Supreme court first ruled it unconstitutional in 1989.[37]

Governor Richards, Lieutenant Governor Bob Bullock, and House Speaker Gib Lewis proposed the new "Fair Share Plan," which included a proposed constitutional amendment that would require that 95 percent of state and local money spent on education be equally distributed among the state's children.[38] It proposed shifting about $400 million in local property tax revenues from school districts with high property wealth to ones with poor property wealth. The state would have reduced its contribution to the system by an equal amount to help fund the property-poor districts. The plan called for a constitutional amendment that would require voter approval. The State Supreme Court gave lawmakers until June 1 to rework the school finance system. In May of 1993, in a typically small turnout, 63 percent of the voters defeated the amendment. Texas District Judge McCown threatened the 1993 legislature, then in session, with a court takeover of the schools. The legislature responded with a law that would take about $450 million in property taxes from 98 high-wealth districts and give it to poor districts. This measure was dubbed the "Robin Hood Law" by the media. In December of 1993, the judge accepted this effort as constitutional. Van de Putte knew, however, that this would not be the last time she would have to deal with the issue of public education funding.

Going into the election year of 1994, Van de Putte's major accomplishment during the 1993 legislative year was landing the downtown campus for the University of Texas at San Antonio (UTSA). In 1993, the Texas Legislature-funded South Texas Border Initiative (which provided $352.4 million for new educational programs and buildings at nineteen universities in the South Texas border region) allocated $71.5 million to UTSA, with $20 million stipulated for the downtown campus. This accomplishment demonstrated that Van de Putte could carry major legislation through both houses. In the 1994 Democratic primary election held March 8, she easily defeated her opponent, Arnulfo Ortiz. Without a Republican challenger in November, she garnered 100 percent of the votes. In a similar manner, Van de Putte's 1996 and 1998 re-election in the primary and general election were uneventful. She went unchallenged both years, winning 100 percent of the votes in the primary and general elections.

One month after the November 1998 election, State Senator Greg Luna, due to kidney disease, other complications from diabetes, and the need for ongoing treatment, decided not to run when his term expired in 2000. State Representatives Robert Puente and Leo Alvarado, both from San Antonio, and Van de Putte announced that they were considering running for the Senate seat, but all mentioned that they would concentrate on the 1999 session for now.[39] This session would not only be Van de Putte's last as a state representative but also her most productive; it set her apart from her potential challengers and provided her with the confidence she needed to successfully run for Luna's seat.

During the 1999 session, in response to high convenience store crimes, Van de Putte attempted to pass several worker safety bills for convenience stores. These bills focused on businesses that sold alcohol and stayed open past midnight. "Some provisions were to have video cameras, lighting directly outside the entrance, and visibility of the cashier from the front of the store," Van de Putte said. The bills failed to pass. However, the public outcry inspired the business community to make these changes and they have since become standard business practices.[40] During this session, House Speaker Pete Laney gave Van de Putte a seat on the House Appropriations Committee. It is a very powerful seat because the committee makes spending decisions. She helped secure $200 million for a new cancer research center in San Antonio (from the state's tobacco settlement) and state financial backing for the 2007 Pan Am Games (although San Antonio eventually lost its bid to Rio de Janeiro, Brazil). She also helped secure assistance for Kelly Air Force Base redevelopment (this base was ordered closed by 2001, stripping almost 20,000 uniformed and civilian employees from the local economy). San Antonio officials formed the Greater Kelly Development Authority in 1996 to offset the impact of the closure. The authority and private companies have successfully converted military maintenance and overhaul hangars for private aviation use.[41]

During this same session, Van de Putte and Representative Toby Goodman, a Republican from Arlington, introduced House Bill 1701 (supported by Southwestern Bell Company, a key corporate powerhouse in San Antonio) that opened the telecommunications market in Texas. It assured customers that local telephone rates would remain the same (freezing Southwestern Bell's rates for basic residential service) and that Southwestern Bell would lower fees paid for long-distance service, thereby passing the savings on to consumers. The bill also increased pricing flexibility so that telephone companies could give customers more benefits through increased competition.[42] The passage of this kind of legislation was important for three reasons. First, Van de Putte was the first Latina to carry a major communications bill in either house. Second, this major legislation was passed even though Van de Putte did not serve on the committee. Third, being able to carry a major communications bill with the support of a powerful business interest showed that she could play with the "big boys" in the Texas Legislature. This success provided her with the momentum she needed to make the transition to the state Senate.

Transferring Experience

After State Senator Greg Luna resigned from office on September 25, 1999, a few months before his term expired, a special election took place in November. Several potential candidates contemplated a run: State Representative Robert Puente, State Representative Leticia Van de Putte, State Representative Leo Alvarado, businessman Mark Weber, lawyer Lauro Bustamante, and consultant Anne Newman.[43] A few days later, Puente announced that he would not be running. Less than a month before the special election, the *San Antonio Express News* recommended Van de Putte for state Senator over her opponents.[44] She also acquired a number of important political endorsements in her bid for the District 26 Texas Senate seat from the Tejano Democrats, San Antonio AFL-CIO, Texas Association of Business Chambers of Commerce, Texans for Lawsuit Reform, National Federation of Independent Businesses, and the Texas Medical Association. In anticipation of Luna's resignation, Van de Putte had already raised $125,000 before he officially resigned.[45]

Among the five candidates, Van de Putte garnered 42 percent of the vote and Alvarado came in second. Because no candidate received a majority, Governor George W. Bush called a runoff between these two candidates. Van de Putte estimates that she spent $250,000 on her campaign.[46] However, a few days after the special election, Alvarado withdrew his candidacy. He cited the close friendship between the two as his reason for withdrawing; he did not wish to put strain on the relationship. Van de Putte responded by saying, "I did not look forward to running against a dear friend. I am thankful for his support and look forward to working with him for the things Bexar County needs. I am honored that he made this decision that benefits both our families and the Democratic Party, as well." Next, Van de Putte had to run in the March 2000 primary and the November general election to retain the seat.[47]

The 2000 Democratic primary was the most competitive race of Van de Putte's political career, and it was the most expensive state Senate race in the history of San Antonio. Her challenger, David McQuade Leibowitz, was a native of the Rio Grande Valley, who began working in farm fields at the age of five to help support his family. He is a San Antonio lawyer who handles personal injury and consumer and workers' rights cases. In his campaign, he promised to provide better access to generic drugs and laws to keep interest rates down, as well as an effort to stop rate increases by the telecommunications industry, including Southwestern Bell.[48] However, Leibowitz had one problem. He did not live in the Senate district in which he wanted to run: He lived in the Dominion Country Club, which was outside Senate District 26. To rectify this problem, he purchased a condominium in the district. Leibowitz had deep pockets and outspent Van de Putte by an estimated three-to-two margin.[49]

The competition turned negative. The two Democrats accused

each other of breaking campaign laws and trying to buy the election with massive spending. Leibowitz accused Van de Putte of being anticonsumer for supporting telecommunications legislation that benefited Southwestern Bell. Van de Putte charged that Leibowitz did not actually live in the mostly inner-city district and that he failed to comply with the state's personal financial disclosure laws.[50] In the end, she carried 54.36 percent to Leibowitz's 45.63 percent of the votes. Leibowitz did not give up his desire for a district seat. In 2004, he ran for state Representative District 117 and won.

In the state of Texas, state Senators serve staggered four-year terms. This means that all members of the body are not selected at the same time, which in turn creates relative stability in the body. When Van de Putte was up for election in 2002, she ran unopposed in the primary and the November election.

Summary

In this chapter we get a glimpse of the political culture, referenced in chapter one, that seeks to maintain the elite male dominated atmosphere in the legislature. Moreover, through the textual analysis of Van de Putte's debate with Simpson and various male legislators we begin to see the broader constraints of the structures of sexism, heterosexism, and paternalism that exist in the electoral political institutions. We also witness her attempts to meander her way through these various constraints while developing into a savvy (and strategic) political player.

Van de Putte's decision to run against all odds in her first race and then to run for a Senate seat indicates cautious calculation and strategizing on her part. Timing was everything to ensure success. Moreover, she waited her turn by not challenging Greg Luna and in return she earned respect from the politicos in San Antonio and from Luna's base of support. She understood the importance of earning community respect and abiding by tradition. More importantly, her communication skills proved instrumental in the art of compromise and got her noticed as a freshman legislator. In addition, she demonstrated enough legislative skill to maneuver major legislation through both houses. Women, particularly Latina women, typically do not carry communication bills, which are considered "masculine." Van de Putte, however, demonstrated that she was quite capable of pushing through such legislation. This earned her the respect of her male colleagues, financial support of big businesses, and the leverage she needed to run for state Senate.

The 2003 legislative year proved to be challenging for Van de Putte and the Texas Democratic Party. The always-contentious affair of state-level redistricting caused walk-outs by Democrats in both state houses and forced Van de Putte into an unprecedented leadership role.

Leticia at age five

Belle, Leticia (age six), and grandmother Lupe Aguilar

Leticia's grandfather's pharmacy, Market Square, San Antonio

Van de Putte family photo for Leticia's first campaign, 1990

State Representative Leticia Van de Putte announces candidacy for State Senate, 1999

FIVE

Symbols and Substance

THEORIZING ABOUT LATINAS LEADING THE LEGISLATURE

IN DECEMBER 1991, one month before the legislative session was to begin, the Democrats were jockeying for the next Speaker of the House. Although the official vote would not occur until January, State Representative Pete Laney (from Hale Center, Texas) had a lock on the Speaker's post. State Representative Jim Rudd (Brownfield, Texas), Laney's main opponent, had already conceded the race. Typically, supporters of the successfully elected Speaker of the House get more favorable committee assignments after the legislature convenes in January. Being a freshman, Van de Putte naively supported Jim Rudd. She was, however, hopeful that Laney would reward hard work with fair committee assignments. "When I serve coffee and sandwiches in the members' lounge, can I have the morning shift?" she joked of her conversation with Laney. In a more serious tone, she said, "He's dealing with individual strength."[1] Van de Putte quickly learned that to be an effective and long-term legislator for her constituents in San Antonio, she had to secure a committee assignment that would allow her to use her strengths.

"I Self-Identified as a Democrat"

Van de Putte was not recruited to the Democratic Party. She became a Democrat because her *padrino* (godfather),[2] State Senator Joe Bernal, was a Democrat. Her political confidant, county commissioner, and *compadre*, Paul Elizondo, was a Democrat. Her husband also was a Democrat. Thus Van de Putte self-identified as a Democrat. In the early 1980s, she did what was expected of Latina women who participated in the party; she hosted tea parties for candidates, block-walked, or helped with the fundraisers and mail-outs. She was a good soldier, but not really part of the party structure.

When Van de Putte first decided to run for office in 1990, she had no party support. The "two darlings were the two front-runners: a trial attorney and a legislative staffer and then three union guys. They were all male and they were coming from very established factions."[3] Certain individuals who were affiliated with the Democratic Party supported her, but the party supported the trial attorney and the legislative staff. Van de Putte explains it this way:

> State Representative Orlando Garcia was extremely supportive. He truly believed in the diversity and he was appalled at the lack of women in the party, legislature, and on boards and commissions. If you look at his record while he was a state representative, he would appoint women to state commissions or advisory boards. He was very sensitive to that and when I think about it . . . He recognized the fact and he thought that gender was a real plus. He also thought it was important to have someone with a health care background and being a mom was a plus. He felt very strongly that the Democratic Party had to have candidates that looked like the people that they were supposed to represent.

Other individuals or trailblazers associated with the party also made it easier for Van de Putte to enter politics, such as Maria Antonietta Berriozábal. In 1981 she became the first Latina to be elected to the San Antonio city council. Irma Rangel (from Kingsville) was the first Latina elected to the state legislature in 1976, and Judith Zaffirini (from Laredo, whose district stretches into San Antonio) was the first Latina elected to the Senate in 1987.

The politics in San Antonio were divided between the northern and southern parts of the city. Southside politics were run by the Tejeda Party and northside politics by the Democratic Party.

The Tejeda Party was known as the "Three Panchos": State Senator (and later Congressman) Frank Tejeda, State Senator Frank Madla, and Frank Wing. They controlled everything that happened with the Democratic Party on the south side of town. The Three Panchos were not active in the Democratic Party, but they had their own political machine. Because Van de Putte was able to garner enough electoral support to win the election without the help of the Democratic Party, she was embraced by the patriarch of the Three Panchos, Frank Tejeda. She had developed her own support base through the various professional organizations in which she participated over the years. Her candor and penchant for doing things her way attracted Tejeda's attention. Tejeda did not really care for the Democratic Party or anyone residing outside of the south side.[4] Van de Putte described a defining moment in their relationship this way: "Frank Tejeda was state senator at the time and he came to the north side. "North side" means anything north of Hildebrand Avenue and I had a campaign fundraiser because the district that I was representing was inner city, Jefferson, right there just north of Hildebrand. I had a fundraiser there . . . lots and lots of people. Frank Tejeda came. Orlando Garcia was still state representative and he said, 'Oh, my God, Senator Tejeda is coming.' And, I said, 'That is so nice for him to come.' He said, 'No, no, you don't understand. He never comes over to north side politics. He stays on the south side. He has never come over here for anything, not for me or for Matt Garcia. The fact that he is here . . . '"

Van de Putte had met Frank Tejeda at the state capital. She had lobbied on behalf of pharmacists for the previous eight years when the state legislature hosted their annual pharmacists for a day, an occasion at which a select group of pharmacists would lobby various state legislators for issues that they deemed important to their interests. On one occasion, Van de Putte had gone to Austin to lobby Tejeda, because he was her state senator, on a very important bill. After their discussion, she thought that Tejeda would vote in support of her bill. She thought that they had his vote and consequently thought that they had all the votes they needed to pass this particular bill. She recalled: “He, on the Senate floor, voted against us. I went back to his office and I said to him, ‘Senator, I am sorry but I thought you had told us you were in support of our bill and I am a little dismayed. Because . . . you know we lost that bill.’ And, he said, ‘Things change. You have to realize things change and I voted in opposition.’ I said, ‘Well, I know that. Why did you lie to me?’ He said, ‘Things change. You have to remember this is politics. It is not just policy.’” After that exchange, Van de Putte did not have any other contact with him until the night of the fundraiser. Van de Putte described the encounter as follows:

> I am the nominee and he comes over to me. Orlando Garcia was on one side and Paul Elizondo was on the other side and they were just amazed that he had come. Frank Tejeda gave me a hug and said, “I am so proud and so thankful. I think you are going to be a great addition to the legislative delegation, is there anything I can do to help you?” I looked him straight in the eyes and I said, “Yes, sir, thank you for coming. The only thing I am going to ever ask of you is to not ever fucking lie to me again.” Orlando’s and Paul’s mouths dropped open. Frank said, “What?” “Don’t ever lie to me again.” He looked at me and said, “Okay.” “That is all I want. If you don’t lie to me, I will be happy.” I gave him a great big hug and a kiss and he started laughing.

Frank Tejeda, Frank Madla, and Irma Rangel were Van de Putte’s mentors, but Tejeda more so than the others because he and Van de Putte commuted together to Austin and back to San Antonio every day during her first term. It was Tejeda who helped stop her from making a lot of mistakes her first year. He taught her how to select a Senate sponsor, how to work the Senate, and whom the key people in the committees were. Tejeda, not the Democratic Party, was very instrumental in Van de Putte’s success as a state representative and politician. With Tejeda taking her under his wing, her base of constituent support and influence grew in both San Antonio and the Texas legislature.

Tejeda also taught Van de Putte the importance of expanding her base in the legislature: to be a person of influence it is necessary be a team player within the institution. He taught her the importance of using her gender, ethnicity, and occupation for political longevity. She needed to understand how such attributes interplay with policy-making and politics. In both the House and Senate, Van de Putte took his advice and immersed herself in the institutional environment. While in the state House of Representatives, Van de Putte served as secretary of the Mexican American Legislative Caucus from 1991 to 1996. From 1998 to 1999, she was vice chair of the caucus, and she temporarily served as chair from February to August of 1998. When she was elected to the state Senate, she served as vice chair from 2000 to 2001 and chair of the Senate's Hispanic Caucus from 2001 to 2003.[5] Since 2003, she has served as chair of the Texas Senate Democratic Caucus and was elected president of the National Hispanic Caucus of State Legislators for 2003 to 2005.[6] Before becoming president of the National Conference of State Legislatures for 2006 to 2007, she served as its vice president from 2005 to 2006.[7] This national visibility has given Van de Putte tremendous political capital.

Committees in Texas

Committees are the "central structural components" of the legislature.[8] As Sinclair argues, "The distribution of valued committee positions provides the single best observable indicator of the distribution of influence in the legislature."[9] Committee assignments are an indication of the institutional power base from which an elected representative operates and are crucial to a representative's daily life and prospects for playing a significant role in policymaking. The positions held by a member of congress are critical in defining the career of a legislator.[10] Not all committees are equally powerful or attractive to representatives. Assignments to committees are typically dictated by party loyalty and seniority, regardless of gender.

During the first week of the legislative session, committee assignments are made. The lieutenant governor and the Speaker of the

House, in their respective chambers, name committee chairmen and announce each panel's membership. The committee announcements occur in late January. Typically, panel posts are filled according to seniority and lawmakers' preference, but the ultimate decision rests with the lieutenant governor and Speaker.

The House has thirty-six standing committees and one special panel. Major committees in the House include Appropriations, Criminal Jurisprudence, Economic Development, Education, Insurance, Rules and Resolutions, and State Affairs or Calendars. The Senate is divided into thirteen committees and two special panels, including Finance, Intergovernmental Relations, International Relations, Trade and Technology, NAFTA (North American Free Trade Agreement), and Health and Human Services. By far the two most powerful and important by constitutional authority are the Finance Committee in the Senate and the Appropriations Committee in the House, both of which are the main bodies through which matters of the budget and taxing are determined. Within the first week of the legislative session, members provide cards indicating their committee preference.

A seat or, even better, a chairmanship on an influential committee increases a lawmaker's stature inside the capitol and can benefit his or her district in various ways. People who want things done, such as lobbyists and constituents, seek out these members. In addition, a chairman, who controls the flow of legislation through his or her committee, has increased bargaining power with other lawmakers. Horse-trading is the name of the game. On the other hand, lawmakers who sit on largely inconsequential "furniture" committees find themselves out of the mainstream on big issues. Too long in such a position can marginalize a political career in a hurry.[11]

In Texas, the advantages held by the majority party in "structuring the committee system, that is, setting up jurisdictions, allocating resources, assigning members, and so forth"[12] has received little attention by analysts. Just as members have individual goals that motivate their legislative behavior, parties have collective goals that motivate leadership behavior. Members are motivated to support the party by a number of external and internal factors, such as committee assignments, legislative support, and campaign funding. In this sense, parties are organizational blocs that cultivate and mobilize support despite individual member and committee interests. Parties have a number of electoral and institutional resources at their disposal to influence member support. This was perhaps most evident in the redistricting efforts in Texas in 2003. By law, the State of Texas must reapportion its districts every ten years in accordance with the U.S. census to account for any population shifts. Because reapportioning occurred in 2000, there was no reason to redraw districts prior to the next census count. However, nothing in the state constitution prevents any party from reapportioning as many times as they wanted. As Texas Republican and U.S. Congressman Tom Delay pushed the Texas legislature to redistrict, Democratic legislators in Texas pushed back by leaving the state and holding out in Albuquerque, New Mexico. This forced Governor Rick Perry to call two special sessions for redistricting just to satisfy what newspapers called "Delay's power grab." In the end, four Democratic districts turned into Republican-leaning districts and Republicans gained five seats in the U.S. House in the 2004 elections, solidifying GOP control of Congress. As House majority leader, Delay wanted to increase the number of Republican elected officials to ensure that President George W. Bush's policy interests were implemented.

A number of factors are considered in making committee assignments, such as the member's expertise, stance on committee-relevant issues, and seniority; the demographic and factional balance of the committee; and the preferences of the chairman (therefore "being in good graces of the party leader is certainly important in getting on major committees"[13]). For the major committees, assignment is restricted to more senior members "who are 'responsible' legislators and who represent districts which do not require them to take inflexible positions on controversial issues."[14] In contrast, "unfavorable assignments, of little political value to the recipients, are sometimes deliberately given by the powers that be as a mark of disapproval, or for reasons that might be described as 'for the good of the order.'"[15]

When it comes to committees in Texas, the importance of each committee weighs on the preferences of the Speaker of the House and the lieutenant governor because they are the most important people in the House and Senate. They guide the direction of policymaking and determine their own priorities on different issues. For example, after the decennial census of 2000, the most important issue in the seventy-seventh legislative session was the redistricting committee. This committee draws new boundaries for House, Senate, congressional, and State Board of Education districts. Then Lieutenant Governor Bill Ratliff named State Senator Judith Zaffirini to that redistricting committee. She was the only Hispanic on the committee, making her a very influential legislator given the priority of the issue and the committee.[16]

In the Senate, all the committees are important because the Senate only has thirty-one members, and they are up for election less frequently than House members. Thus they have to work with each other more than do House members, and it is difficult to dismiss someone because one may need his or her support later. In the House, committee appointments depend on what the Speaker values, who he or she sees as confidantes and policy players, and the important issues for the session. Given the size of the House—150 members—and the frequency with which they are elected, the Speaker has more wiggle room than the lieutenant governor for placing members on committees that are not critical to the person's home base. For example, a member's committees should relate to the needs of his or her district, thereby making that member even more powerful because he or she can deliver on promises by using muscle in those respective committees. Some members get punished with "bad" or "powerless" committee appointments because they have done something against the leadership, violated some rule, or have fallen in disfavor with the leadership. For example, if a legislator who represents the big city of Houston is assigned to the Agriculture Committee, then he or she is in a bind. He or she would be forced to negotiate deals with other committees that deal with issues important to Houston by assuring them that he or she will pass something for them if they pass something for him or her.

In the House, some committees are considered more important than others, given the industry and politics of the state.[17] Early in her career, Van de Putte was placed on furniture committees. However, as the political climate changed, she served on committees that dealt with timely issues (see table 1), thereby increasing her level of importance and influence. For example, in 1997 she served on the Insurance Committee, which was instrumental in the passage of the Patient Protection Act. This bill gave women, regardless of their insurance carrier, the right to choose their own obstetrician or gynecologist. This was a blow to insurance companies that required women to get a referral from their primary care physician. In addition, Van de Putte was placed on the House Appropriations Committee during her last year as a state representative. Since she has been in the Senate, she has yet to be placed on the powerful Finance Committee. However, her senate colleague, Judith Zaffirini served as vice chair of finance during the 2005 regular session.

Van de Putte's appointments have had a direct connection to the needs of San Antonio. San Antonio's economic sustenance depends on education, the military, and business. These connections alone make her a very valuable and powerful legislator. Education funding is always a critical issue for Texas, particularly in the post–Robin Hood era. As of the 2005 legislative session, Van de Putte was a member of the Education Committee, so she was part of the 2006 special session in which the State of Texas restructured the way it funds its public schools. Being a part of this committee was a big deal, particularly because the committee considered a business tax on corporations to fund public schools. Van de Putte is also the chair of the Veteran Affairs and Military Installations Committee, which is an influential position given San Antonio's military community and because as chair she controls the type of legislation and flow of legislation for that committee.

TABLE 1

Leticia Van de Putte's committee membership in the Texas state legislature

Legislative session	Van de Putte's committees
72nd Regular Session—1991 (House)	Human Services Labor & Employment Relations, Select Rules
73rd Regular Session—1993	Human Services International & NAFTA & GATT Special Select Cultural Affairs
74th Regular Session—1995	Economic Development Juvenile Justice and Family Issues State Loans and Grants House Joint
75th Regular Session—1997	Economic Development Economic Development Subcommittee on Welfare & Workforce Reform Insurance (*Vice Chair*)
76th Regular Session—1999	Appropriations Economic Development (*Vice Chair*) Education Jurisprudence Veteran Affairs & Military Installations
77th Regular Session—2001 (Senate)	Business & Commerce Education Natural Resources Public Interest Counsel Business & Commerce Committee on Prevailing Wage Rates (*Chair*) Business & Commerce Subcommittee on the Termination of Contractual Agreements Between Insurers and Insurance Agents
78th Regular Session—2003	Administration Business Education Veteran Affairs & Military Installations (*Chair*) Subcommittee on Higher Education Public School Finance, Select

(Table 1, continued)

Legislative session	Van de Putte's committees
79th Regular Session—2005	Administration Business & Commerce Education Veteran Affairs and Military Installations (*Chair*)
80th Regular Session—2007	Business & Commerce Committee of the Whole Senate Education State Affairs Veteran Affairs and Military Installations (*Chair*)

To become influential, a legislator does not have to be part of a major committee to sponsor major legislation. Van de Putte found this to be true in 1999. Although she "wasn't on the committee that heard Telecom, [she] was the co-author of the Telecom bill, a major, major state bill." Van de Putte was very strategic in how she handled this bill. She said, "I knew I could not get it passed without a very good technician so I asked Toby Goodman. . . . [He] is a precise technician and a lawyer and I knew that he wasn't going to have anything to do with it. I said, 'C'mon we can do this.' He replied, 'But, I don't know anything about this.' 'You can learn. It will be fun.' So, it was a team effort." It did not bother Van de Putte that Goodman was a Republican. She believed that the bill was good for Texas and that it was important to look past partisan differences. Being able to develop working relations across party lines and push this bill through both houses without being on the committee garnered the attention of the business interests and gave her the confidence to run for state Senate in a special election later that year. She demonstrated a unique leadership skill, one that fosters cooperation and collaboration.

On its own, being a skilled policymaker does not win re-election. Success requires being able to form relationships and a connectedness with constituents. *Personalismo* is particularly important for Van de Putte and her constituents. She learned from Tejeda, and the way in which he ran southside politics, how important it is for the community to believe they have a real connection to their representatives. To accomplish this, Van de Putte integrates what the political science literature calls symbolic and substantive legislation.

Substantive and Symbolic Legislation

Much of the legislation initiated in Congress can be labeled symbolic. Symbolic legislation translates into symbolic representation. Valeria Sinclair Chapman defined symbolic legislation as "legislation sponsored with the objective of giving psychological reassurance to constituents that representatives are working in their interests and are responsive to their needs."[18] This is the same for substantive legislation, which translates into substantive representation. Substantive representation means having a "representative with congruent policy views acting as an advocate."[19] Mexican American legislators provide Hispanic constituents with the greatest amount of symbolic representation. They understand the importance of *personalismo*, and they also initiate and participate in providing their Hispanic constituents with policies of substance, namely those that distribute or redistribute tangible public goods. Legislative success needs to be evaluated on a broader plan than how previous scholars have defined it. Whether one considers symbolic legislation important or not, members of Congress in general spend a great deal of energy providing it to constituents. In the end, Hispanic legislators have limited power because they are in the minority, but they can still influence policy through symbolic legislation.

More instances of symbolic representation than substantive representation have always passed through the Texas legislature during any given regular session. For example, in the Seventy-second regular legislative session, in 1991, state lawmakers passed 2,216 pieces of symbolic legislation and 960 pieces of substantive legislation.[20] For the Seventy-ninth regular legislative session, in 2005, 3,581 pieces of symbolic legislation passed compared to 1,389 pieces of substantive legislation.[21] In the Eightieth regular legislative session, in 2007, 1,480 pieces of substantive legislation passed and 4,360 pieces of symbolic legislation made its way through both houses. Below are some examples of symbolic resolutions that Van de Putte filed:

1. House Concurrent Resolution 105: In memory of Dr. Saul Severino Trevino.
2. H. Resolution 989: Honoring Christi Cano of Edison High School in San Antonio for winning the 1999 UIL Class 4A state individual golf title.
3. H. C. Resolution 161: Urging Congress to change veterans' mortgage bonds to cover all veterans who have served on active duty.
4. H. C. Resolution 202: Designating May 1, 2003, as Law Day in the State of Texas.

Three types of symbolic policies exist: concurrent resolution, joint resolution, and simple resolution. Concurrent resolutions are a type of legislative measure that requires passage by both chambers of the legislature and generally requires action by the governor. A concurrent resolution is used to convey the sentiment of the legislature and may offer a commendation, a memorial, a statement of congratulations, a welcome, or a request for action by another governmental entity. A joint resolution is a type of legislative measure that requires passage by both chambers of the legislature but does not require action by the governor. A joint resolution is used to propose amendments to the Texas constitution, to ratify amendments to the U.S. Constitution, or to request a convention to propose amendments to the U.S. Constitution. Before becoming effective, the provisions of joint resolutions proposing amendments to the Texas constitution must be approved by the voters of Texas. Finally, a simple resolution is a resolution that is considered only within the chamber in which it is filed. It can offer commendation, a memorial, a statement of congratulations, a welcome, or another statement of legislative sentiment.

Symbolic policies are still public policies, but of a different sort than most. In general, public policies are classified according to the kinds of objectives or results they seek. Scholars generally agree that public policies with domestic (as opposed to foreign) policy objectives seek to regulate the behavior of individuals and corporations; protect consumers; foster competition in the corporate marketplace; redistribute wealth, property, or legally prescribed advantages; or protect civil rights among classes of people or ethnic groups. Symbolic policies do not distribute or redistribute any public good or regulate anything in the standard sense; instead, they reflect their constituents' interests and concerns. Most concretely, symbolic legislation can:

- provide political cover, to conceal a voting record that otherwise could be interpreted as contrary to the objectives of the symbolic bill,
- initiate or augment a larger political objective or agenda,
- persuade fellow members on core principles before specific bills are introduced,
- cultivate support in the Texas legislature,
- speak to and address the concerns of groups and constituents that otherwise would not get addressed.[22]

William Morrow, a scholar of government, contended that the three standard types of policy—distributive, regulatory, and redistributive—engage different types of politics.[23] Symbolic resolutions are debated and legislated differently as well. Distributive policies, for example, are generally very popular because they distribute public goods—like price supports for farmers and contracts for defense suppliers—to a vast array of groups. Of course, distributive policies become more controversial in times of fiscal stress. Because regulatory policies are technical and normally apply to a small set of individuals or groups, they are less public, although the politics surrounding them can be as fierce as those surrounding redistributive policies. In contrast, symbolic resolutions and bills that confer symbolic recognition on groups (for example, designating post offices after community leaders and known ethnic or racial leaders) very often are passed through a suspension of the rules. Noncontroversial bills, those "narrow in impact or minor in importance," are generally considered under a suspension of rules.[24] Although a floor vote usually occurs, debate is generally limited to forty minutes, and the vote is sometimes taken by voice only. Furthermore, no amendments are allowed, and a two-thirds vote is required for passage. The rules are designed to speed up the process, prevent obstructionism, and save time. In this way, a symbolic resolution is exceptionally easy to pass, and its passage is often hidden from full view of the media and the American public.

The American political system has a distributive policy bias: policies that distribute small goods across a wide array of groups and interests are more likely to be passed than those redistributing assets or those regulating a business. In this way, symbolic resolutions are like distributive public policies. Symbolic policies do not cost taxpayers much, if anything. Thus, symbolic policies are a cheap way to distribute some immaterial public goods to constituents.

A comparison of Van de Putte's legislative history during her freshman legislative session with that of other House Latinas (see appendix 2) elected or serving at the same time shows that Van de Putte ranks at the low end of producing substantive legislation,[25] while at the same time ranking among the top submitters of symbolic legislation. During her last legislative session, in 1999, she ranked among the top two producers of substantive legislation. As Van de Putte matured into a seasoned politician, she began to understand the political importance of community connectedness: the best way to maintain this connectedness, and seem influential in the process to the ordinary constituent, was by passing symbolic legislation.

As a state senator for the seventy-seventh regular session in 2001, Van de Putte co-sponsored 58 House bills, of which 44 became effective, and submitted 87 Senate bills, of which 17 became effective. In contrast, Judith Zaffirini (a Democrat from Laredo) submitted 37 House bills and 72 Senate bills, of which 31 and 31, respectively, became effective. When Van de Putte was reelected to the seventy-eighth regular legislative session in 2003, she cosponsored 28 House bills, of which 21 became effective, and submitted 86 Senate bills, with 21 effective. Zaffirini cosponsored 22 House bills with 17 effective and 102 Senate bills with 20 effective. By the eightieth regular legislative session in 2007 Van de Putte submitted 111 Senate bills with only 20 becoming effective and sponsoring 36 House bills with only 30 becoming effective. Zaffirini submitted 79 Senate bills with 23 becoming effective and sponsoring 48 house bills with 42 becoming effective (for a tabular representation of the above information, see appendix 2). Thus, Van de Putte appears to be a savvy senator, which reflects her experience and understanding of "how to work the legislature."

Summary

Van de Putte's skill as a legislator was influenced by one of San Antonio's own political machines, Frank Tejeda. Her association with Tejeda gave her unsolicited constituent support for a future run at state senate. Perhaps most importantly, Tejeda began honing her leadership skills. He taught Van de Putte that policymaking is inextricably linked to politics. Policies change according to the political climate. Understanding the political culture of the state was important for policy. The building of relationships with her colleagues and constituents is necessary for political longevity. It is not about challenging the system (via ethnicity or gender) but having the political acumen to know how to maneuver within the system. For example, Van de Putte understood that developing relationships with key individuals was necessary to advance public policy and preserve one's longevity as a state legislator. From Tejeda, Van de Putte learned how to select a cosponsor in the senate (for any bill to pass both houses, it needs a cosponsor). Partisanship is less important than good public policy. In addition, she learned to become an institutional party player by assuming various positions in state and national caucuses. Moreover, Van de Putte learned that to maintain constituent connectedness, symbolic legislation is important when it comes to perceptions of influence. The absence of symbolic legislation would contribute to the symbolic marginalization or perception of exclusion of one's constituents. Furthermore, she learned that a legislator's power and influence depends on membership in particular committees, the important of which is determined by the issues facing the state at any particular time. These experiences prepared Van de Putte for the biggest partisan battle of her career.

SIX

The Illusion of Inclusion Revisited

2003 PROVED TO BE one of the most politically controversial years in the history of Texas politics. Eleven senate Democrats learned that they were not included in Republican Governor Rick Perry's and the Texas legislature's quest to redraw district lines to increase Republican delegation for Texas in Washington. The eleven state senators were: Gonzalo Barrientos (Austin, Dist. 14), Rodney Ellis (Houston, Dist. 13), Mario Gallegos Jr. (Houston, Dist. 6), Juan "Chuy" Hinojosa (McAllen, Dist. 6), Eddie Lucio Jr. (Brownsville, Dist. 27), Frank Madla (San Antonio, Dist. 19), Eliot Shapleigh (El Paso, Dist. 29), Royce West (Dallas, Dist. 23), John Whitmire (Houston, Dist. 15), Letitica Van de Putte (San Antonio, Dist. 26), and Judith Zaffirini (Laredo, Dist. 21). According to Democrats, prior to the redistricting showdown of 2003 the bipartisan effort by the GOP-controlled state legislature gave the illusion of inclusion when it came to creating policy for the good of Texas, but their mid-decade actions toward redistricting were clearly partisan. Democrats responded by initiating a protest that would change the dynamics of state politics for forty-five days.

The Seeds for Protest Had Already Been Planted

During the regular spring session in May 2003, the Republicans tried to push redistricting toward a vote in the GOP-controlled state House. In response, fifty-one Democrats from that chamber fled across the state line to a Holiday Inn in Ardmore, Oklahoma, to block a quorum,[1] thereby killing the bill. When the House Democrats fled to Oklahoma, Republican House Speaker Tom Craddick ordered state troopers (Texas Department of Public Safety, or DPS) to find them and bring them back to Austin. Representative Lon Burnam (a Democrat from Fort Worth) sued Craddick, saying Craddick's deployment of the troopers was an abuse of power. District Judge Charles Campbell ruled that the Texas DPS lacks the legal authority to arrest state House members who break a quorum.[2] Two and a half months later, eleven of the state Senate's twelve Democrats (the "Texas Eleven" or "Killer D's") broke quorum and fled on two private jets to the Marriott Pyramid North in Albuquerque, New Mexico.

The Texas legislature is no stranger to broken quorums. In April 1993, Republicans (the "Killer WASPS") shut down the Senate for one day when they left the chamber to avoid a vote on the judicial selection plan designed to increase the number of minority judges in nine urban counties. The proposal resulted from federal court rulings stating that the current countywide system discriminated against black and Hispanic voters because white bloc voting prevented minority-backed candidates from winning elections. Democrats later agreed to send the measure back to committee.[3] The difference then was that the state had no valid district map and needed one; in 2003, the state had a valid map that was approved by the U.S. Supreme Court, and even the Republican attorney general of Texas had ruled that the legislature was under no obligation to redistrict in 2003.[4] The flight to New Mexico in July was the second time in 2003 that Democratic lawmakers left the capital to block a Republican plan to redraw the boundaries of the state's thirty-two congressional districts.

In May 1979, a group of legislators clashed with then Lieutenant Governor Bill Hobby and prevailed. This incident, known as "the attack of the Killer Bees," has assumed the status of legend in Texas politics. It all began late in the legislative session when Hobby tried to push through the Senate a bill that would establish separate-day presidential and state primary elections. He hoped this change would enable conservative Democrats to vote for former Texas governor and Republican presidential hopeful John Connally in a Republican presidential primary before returning to the regular state Democratic primary to choose candidates for state offices. However, Hobby could not bring the bill up for consideration because twelve senators refused to vote to suspend the two-thirds rule to do so. Suspending the rule would have meant that Hobby did not need two-thirds of the Senate to consider the bill, but that a simple majority would do. In a rare fit of pique, Hobby announced that he was going to supersede the rules and bring up the bill anyway. In response, the twelve senators disappeared and the Senate ground to a standstill for lack of a quorum. Furious, Hobby invoked his power as lieutenant governor, ordering the DPS and the Texas Rangers to begin an all-out search for the missing senators. Word spread quickly, and soon the media joined in the hunt for the wayward twelve, fueling rumors of "sightings" all over the state. Under increasing pressure from other senators, Hobby finally relented and announced that the dual primary bill was dead for the session. The twelve wayward senators, given assurances that they would not face retaliation for their actions, returned in triumph to the Senate chamber and the session ended without further incident. Rarely can individual legislators challenge the power of a presiding officer and win.

The Texas Eleven

By the end of the 2003 legislative session in May, State Senator Gonzalo Barrientos decided that he had had enough of being the chair of the Democratic Caucus, a position he had held since 1999. Van de Putte began receiving a number of phone calls from her Senate Democratic colleagues encouraging her to take the position. By this time, Van de Putte had made a name for herself as someone who had good communication skills and was good at forging working relationships with other senators. They would say, "You need to take over as chair." She replied, "I am the newest one of the bunch." "No, no, no, you need to take over as chair. We are facing redistricting. You need to be chair."[5] After much negotiation, she finally decided to assume the position of Democratic chair under certain conditions.

The first condition was that she would not make decisions unilaterally. "Everybody is at the table making the decisions. But, once the decisions are made, I am the enforcer, and I have to have backup from everybody in the room on that, but the decisions are made collectively."[6] The second condition was that in the event the Senate broke quorum, which she knew they would, she would have sole responsibility and sole say-so over all logistics. "All logistics, because you cannot have a committee decide that. I would have sole authority from them to negotiate all logistics. And that they would not know [details], nor would I tell them until it was absolutely necessary. They did not know our destination until we got on the plane."[7]

No one knew when Van de Putte was going to order the senators to break quorum—not her husband and not the pilots that were going to fly the senators to their destination. The night before their escape, Van de Putte said that she became "really nervous" about what Texas Republicans were planning. As a precaution, she implemented a contingency plan with the help of Senator Juan Hinojosa that brought two private jet aircraft to Austin and that alerted the drivers of vans that were to carry lawmakers to the airport to be ready to move at a moment's notice. The eleven senators fled after a first special session called by the governor to address redistricting drew to a close. One plane was owned by Joe La Mantia, a McAllen beer distributor, and the other by David Rogers, an Edinburg banker.[8] Within two hours of the close of the first special session, Governor Perry called a second session. By this time the Texas Eleven were airborne. The pilots were unsure where they were going. Van de Putte initially told the pilots to file the flight plan for Amarillo, Texas. Twenty minutes into the flight, she informed the pilots of their new flight destination: Albuquerque, New Mexico.[9] The office of the U.S. House majority leader, Tom DeLay, a Texas Republican, got involved, calling the Federal Aviation Administration to locate the plane that the Democrats used.[10] This action caused political observers to question whether or not DeLay abused his power. DeLay dismissed such scrutiny, but this marked the beginning of the end of DeLay's political career. He would later be indicted by Austin's district attorney, Ronny Earl, for his involvement in the Republican redistricting effort.

On July 29, two days after the Democrats broke quorum, the Republican redistricting plan passed the House and was sent to the Senate, which remained in recess pending the return of eleven of its twelve Democratic members. When House Speaker Tom Craddick gaveled the chamber to session that morning, it was unable to proceed due to lack of a quorum. Craddick dispatched staffers to round up enough Democrats to allow the House to be gaveled into session. Democratic state representatives tried in vain to slow down the Republican majority. They delayed a quorum for three hours by being tardy. Each special session costs approximately $1.7 million.[11]

The Texas Stand Off

The House members' Oklahoma motel caper just a couple of months earlier had attracted national attention and was seen as the latest example of the often-colorful politics in Texas. However, the redistricting standoff had moved into an ominous new phase for the Democrats. Van de Putte and the other senators left Austin at the start of the second, thirty-day special legislative session that had been called to deal with redistricting, leaving behind families, friends, and their regular jobs.

The stakes in the standoff had national implications. Democrats held a seventeen-to-fifteen advantage in the state's U.S. House delegation but risked losing five or more of those seats in the November 2006 elections if Republicans redrew the district lines. Such a shift in power in Washington would cement the Republican's House majority for at least the rest of the decade and enhance the prospects of then-Majority Leader Tom Delay, who was seen as the driving force behind the redistricting plan. Underscoring the importance of the battle was some speculation that Karl Rove, President Bush's chief political strategist, had discussed tactics with Lieutenant Governor David Dewhurst, also a Republican and the presiding officer in the State Senate. Rove also became involved in Colorado, where the legislature shifted congressional boundaries in the spring of 2002 to solidify Republican support in two districts. On July 15, 2003, *The Monitor* confirmed communication on redistricting between Rove and Dewhurst. In that same month, a White House spokesman said Rove had been in touch with at least one Texas legislator about redistricting.[12] This was beginning to resemble an outright power grab.

The Republican's argument for redrawing the state's congressional districts was that the current lines did not fairly reflect the state's increasingly Republican tilt. In 2003, no Democrats held a statewide office and Republicans had a majority in both state chambers, yet Texas Democrats outnumbered Republicans seventeen to fifteen in the U.S. House. After the legislature deadlocked on redistricting in 2001, Governor Perry deferred to the courts, an option which was within his constitutional discretion, knowing that doing so would result in judicial determinations. A panel of three federal judges (two were Republican) came up with the current districts. The U.S. Supreme Court upheld the Republican panel that created the plan. The final redistricting map would elect as many as twenty-one Republicans to Congress. "Clearly, no one is going to dispute the fact that this would help President Bush to send people who would more closely defend this agenda," said Ted Delisi, a GOP consultant in Austin.[13] Van de Putte's account supports this claim:

> We didn't hear about redistricting until about April 2003 when the president's numbers started to go down and until Tom Delay started making the visits and that Karl Rove started putting pressure. I saw a difference in rhetoric from Republicans who said (about redistricting) "Like the flu, don't even want to go there. Not necessary to . . ." Well, if the House deals with it, the Senate will look at it. If the House sends us a bill the Senate will look at it, which was kind of late spring to May, which is when the rhetoric changed: "You know the majority of Texans agree with

> President Bush's policies and the majority of the Texas Congressional Delegation does not. We need more people to support the President." You know, so it was a power grab. It was a power grab, plain and simple. What scares me is that if any party or group of people can't win an issue under regular circumstances, regular Senate rules, that they change the terms of the engagement and change things at any cost so that they do win.[14]

The Democrats knew they were still safe because of the rules and traditions of the Texas Senate. Under normal Senate procedures, each session begins with the introduction of a "blocker bill," a measure of no significance that is placed at the top of the agenda. The device has the effect of creating a permanent, institutionalized filibuster, requiring a two-thirds vote to suspend the rules to consider any other legislation. With twelve of the Senate's thirty-one seats, the Democrats were able to block consideration of the Republican redistricting plan during the first special session. However, Dewhurst made it clear that there would be no blocker bill if Perry called a second special session, which meant that only the lack of a two-thirds quorum could prevent the Senate from acting. Then, a simple majority would decide the issue. Van de Putte and other Democrats scoff at that argument. Democrats still controlled the Texas House in 2001, and the deadlock over redistricting threw the issue into federal court. Van de Putte claimed that Republicans used the blocker bill device in 2001 to prevent Senate consideration of redistricting legislation.

The Democrat's position was that the end result of Tom Delay's vision of redistricting would be a "resegregation" of sorts. They suggested that Delay wanted the Republican Party to be the party of Anglos. The Democrats would represent mostly low-income people of color clustered on the U.S.-Mexico border and in the inner city. Van de Putte argued that the "Republicans were using a technique called 'pack and crack' where minorities are packed into districts and then you crack the rest of them into districts where they are going to be insignificant because they are not going to have any influence in picking the person who represents them."[15] The Texas Eleven believed Republicans were disenfranchising their minority constituents.

Democrats believed that this was a power grab because of the lieutenant governor's flip-flop on the issue. From January to July 2003, Lieutenant Governor Dewhurst did an about-face on the issue of redistricting. On January 30, the *Dallas Morning News* reported that Dewhurst remarked that "Congressional redistricting is almost as attractive as contagious flu" to a panel of Texas editorial writers in Austin. "The Senate won't take up the idea," he said, "unless it comes over from the House in a form that will attract both a two-thirds vote in the Senate (21 votes) and the support of Hispanic interest groups." On February 26, the *Fort-Worth Star-Telegram* reported Dewhurst as saying, "There are more pressing matters, such as the state budget and reforming home owners insurance that are going to take up a lot of the Senate's side" (in reference to redistricting). On June 10, the *Houston Chronicle* reported that Dewhurst was unenthusiastic about taking up redistricting because he considered it politically divisive. Dewhurst's position was that redistricting could increase partisan rancor to the detriment of other important issues, such as school finance. Moreover, the idea of Republicans gaining congressional seats to reflect their strength among Texas voters would destroy the bipartisanship he worked for during his first session as lieutenant governor. However, the *Associated Press State and Local Wire* confirmed that U.S. House Majority Leader Tom Delay and other congressmen had visited Dewhurt, and shortly thereafter, Dewhurst changed his mind. On July 16 the *Star-Telegram* reported that "Dewhurst told the Associated Press on Monday that if it becomes clear that the 21 votes needed to bring the House redistricting bill up for debate aren't available, he would 'consider all of our options.' That could include the Senate rule." The Texas Eleven believed their options were limited.

While the Republicans were strategizing, the Senate Democrats were consulting lawyers, such as Gerry Hebert, who gave them notebooks before they left for Albuquerque. These notebooks contained information on their legal rights as state legislators acting outside of state chambers. For example, the senators were to consult the notebooks in the event that they were arrested by Texas law enforcement officers. One potential scenario was the following: "The first response of a Senator to a law enforcement officer should be: 'Am I being arrested?' If the answer is 'yes,' then the law enforcement officer should be informed that the Texas Constitution does not authorize a senator to be arrested in traveling to and from the Senate. If the law enforcement official says 'no' and that they are not there to arrest only to accompany, then they need to be informed that no accompaniment is necessary or desired."[16] Any step senators made and anything they wrote for public release or filed was reviewed and pre-approved by their attorney. They had to be careful because they knew a court challenge was inevitable.

Van de Putte knew that they were about to incur a heavy financial burden. She began to strategize for a costly fight. First, she assigned some of the senators the task of fund-raising for their possible litigation fund, which meant that they would have to travel. The goal was to raise soft money. Soft money, including corporate funds and union dues, may be used for litigation because it is not a campaign-related activity. The objective was to raise $600,000 for the litigation budget.[17]

Second, Van de Putte announced that the Texas Eleven had started a grassroots effort to raise money. Shapleigh and Barrientos, who could travel away from Albuquerque on speaking engagements to raise money, did so.[18] The web-based group, MoveOn.org, launched television ads and radio spots to criticize a White House-backed plan to redraw Texas congressional districts. Van de Putte was quick to acknowledge that "while these are not our ads, they were placed in our behalf." By August 23, the Texas Eleven had received about $850,000, with the average contribution about $30.[19] By September 4, MoveOn.org had raised over $1 million for the Texas Eleven.[20]

The Texas Eleven knew that they had to continue their battle with the Republicans for public opinion via the media. Three days into the standoff, Dewhurst said, "I told them that quite frankly if they went to a vacation spot they would lose the public relations battle even more."[21]

Van de Putte had to maintain public support and bring continued media attention to their efforts. She had to keep the plight of the Texas Eleven in the public view. She was concerned that they would lose public momentum because the 2003 California recall was occurring at the same time. This recall garnered unprecedented media attention because of who was challenging then Governor Gray Davis, a Democrat: actor-turned-politician Arnold Schwarzenegger, a Republican. For every day the Texas Eleven were in Albuquerque, by eight o'clock in the morning Van de Putte had done two radio shows back in Texas and two on-camera interviews.[22] She and her colleagues, like Zaffirini, also briefed the reporters daily as to the number of days they had been in Albuquerque and the specific issue they would focus on for that day. The message was clear. Even though they were not in Austin, the senators were still dealing with issues that were important to Texans. For example, Van de Putte noted just how costly the DeLay power grab was by saying, "To update you, today is day eight and the hardworking taxpayers of Texas will pay yet another $57,000 to finance Rick Perry's misguided efforts to satisfy Tom DeLay's partisan power grab. For the record, we should note that $57,000 would pay for 41 Texas children to be put back on the Children's Health Insurance Program for a full year. The costs are mounting, and we'll be updating you on a daily basis on the price Texans are being forced to pay for Rick Perry's misplaced priorities."[23] Governor Perry struck back with his own commercial mantra: "$36 million of the $167 million would be used for community care services if the Democrats were doing their job."[24] State Senator Mario Gallegos, one of the "Killer D's," shot back by saying, "If health and human services are truly the priority of the governor, then he will immediately take redistricting off the table." Perry responded by saying, "That is like negotiating for hostages." Gallegos responded, "Legislative action is not required to allocate the health care funds cited as threatened by Perry because the Governor and the Legislative Budget Board already have that authority."[25] Republican Attorney General Greg Abbott later confirmed what Democrats had said all along: Perry and the Legislative Budget Board already had the power to spend new federal money on health care if they wanted to do so.

In another example, the Texas Eleven took advantage of a political opportunity made available to them by one of their constituents. Van de Putte began one morning briefing by saying, "Today is day nine of Rick Perry's second partisan special session. Today another $57,000 of Texas taxpayers' money will be wasted. That's $57,000 that could go toward restoring the governor's spiteful, vengeful cut of job training funds to the GI Forum."[26] The American GI veterans group argued that Perry "angrily canceled a scheduled appearance at the group's annual national meeting." The GI Forum, which claims 6,000 members in Texas, came under fire from Republicans the summer of 2003 after leaders organized Texans to testify against Perry's decision to call a special session to redraw the state's thirty-two congressional districts. Later the GI Forum said, "Perry retaliated by denying the group a $300,000 grant to maintain a national veterans outreach program that helps veterans find jobs."[27] One week later, however, Governor Rick Perry announced a $300,000 grant for the American GI Forum.

The senators understood the importance of maintaining their momentum back in Texas. On August 9, on the south steps of the state capitol in Austin, Texas, the Texas Eleven held their first rally. The theme was "Enough is Enough/Ya Basta." The state of Texas had been divided into eight regions, with the local congressional members responsible for recruiting rally attendees and providing transportation to Austin. The regions were North Texas, Northeast Texas, Southeast Texas, Houston, Central/West Texas, South Texas, and Austin.[28] For this rally, Democratic senators were given a "secret" telephone number to use so that they could speak at the rally. They were warned, however, that "if the number gets out and Republicans infiltrate they'll shut it down and no senators will be able to talk." Van de Putte was the only member of the Texas Eleven to have that number.[29] About 5,000 people attended the rally and it cost about $68,980.48 (costs included fees and site preparation, promotional ads, lunches, water, snacks, buses, robo calls[30] and phone banks).

The Republican leadership, with the approval of State Attorney General Gregg Abbott and in accordance with the state constitution, imposed penalties and fines on the absent Democrats to compel their attendance. On August 13, Van de Putte made the following statement: "Yesterday afternoon Republicans in the Texas Senate, without a quorum, levied a shameful and illegal poll tax on the Texas Eleven. In so doing, these white Republicans have levied a poll tax on every minority member of the Texas Senate. The Republicans demanded $57,000 per senator. Ironically, this is the identical amount that Rick Perry's special sessions on redistricting are costing taxpayers per day. Here's an idea—call off these redistricting sessions, we'll forget about the fines, and we'll call it even. This isn't just a poll tax on us. It is a poll tax on our constituents. It is an illegal poll tax on the 1.4 million minority Texans they seek to disenfranchise through their partisan redistricting scheme."[31] Van de Putte's response to the imposed penalties honed in on three themes for the constituents of Texas. First, the sanctions created a second class of senators "whose constituents cannot be well served under this official oppression." Second, the request that the penalties be paid in full was equivalent to a poll tax. Third, the penalties were illegal because the senators did not have a quorum to authorize the penalties.[32] The senators who remained in Austin imposed additional penalties on the missing senators:

> A penalty of $1,000 per day, doubling each day, not to exceed $5,000 per day, for each member of the Senate absent from the second called session of the 78th Legislature. . . . To ensure payment of penalties imposed on the absent senators to compel their attendance, the Secretary of the Senate is hereby directed to suspend the provision of the following privileges to senators absent from the second called session of the 78th Legislature until the said penalties be paid in full: all purchasing privileges; all mail privileges limited to $200 per month in postage; all travel; no

> reservations for conference rooms, press conference rooms, or meeting rooms will be allowed; all parking privileges for senators and staff; all subscriptions; all printing privileges including newsletter production; all cell phones; floor passes for staff of delinquent members.[33]

These penalties would later be reduced to mere "probation." However, the motion of probation was mysteriously coy about the names of the senators under probation, perhaps finessing the problem of how to distinguish Senator John Whitmire (the lone senator to leave the Texas Eleven) from the rest of his Democratic colleagues.[34] Whitmire's involvement will be discussed later in the chapter.

Another strategy to keep the plight of the Democratic senators in the media was to have family members of each of the senators in Albuquerque show their support by making speeches in each of their respective home bases in Texas. This occurred periodically throughout the Texas Eleven's stay in Albuquerque. It served as a constant reminder not only to their constituents but also to Texans in general as to why they fled to Albuquerque. The speeches emphasized several themes: 1) that the senators were fighting not only for minority rights, but also for voter rights; 2) that Governor Rick Perry and Lieutenant Governor Dewhurst changed the long-standing Senate rules; and 3) that the leadership ability of the eleven senators was important for protecting voter rights.

While a very public fight was being played out in the media, attorneys for both sides were battling it out in the courts. By the second week of August, the eleven Democrats filed a federal lawsuit alleging violations of the Voting Rights Act, and the Texas Supreme Court denied the GOP's request to order the eleven runaway Democrats back to the Senate chamber.[35] The Texas Senate Democrats also sought a federal judge's order preventing the lieutenant governor from changing a senate rule that blocked passage of a redistricting bill. Political science professor Cal Jillson of Southern Methodist University said the lawsuit idea "seems hopeless to me" because federal courts do not intervene in legislative processes but "only evaluate the results."[36] On August 20, the twenty-fourth day in Albuquerque, Van de Putte unveiled new information to the press about the Republican efforts at redistricting, years prior to Dewhurst's ascendance to the position of lieutenant governor. In a press release, she made the following statement:

> First, we learned, by accident, that while the Republican Attorney General denies to a federal court that removal of the two-thirds rule is subject to approval by the U.S. Department of Justice, the Republican Secretary of State is secretly petitioning the Department of Justice for the very approval they deny is needed. Second, Republican Senator Bill Ratliff, the elder statesman of the Texas Senate and former lieutenant governor, disclosed that Tom DeLay has been trying to manipulate Congressional redistricting in Texas for more than two years. DeLay pressured then-Lieutenant Governor Ratliff to remove the two-thirds rule so they could pass their unfair, partisan redistricting plan. Fair-minded statesman that he is, the lieutenant governor refused. Why? Because unlike Rick Perry, David Dewhurst, and Tom Craddick, Senator Ratliff prioritizes the needs of Texas over those of the Republican Party. Politics ranks last in Bill Ratliff's world, as it should in the state Republican leadership.[37]

To counter these efforts by the Republicans, the congressional districts in Texas wrote a letter to Voting Rights Section Chief Joseph Rich of the in the U.S. Department of Justice. The Texas Congressional delegates were reminding Rich not to succumb to the partisan pressure of the Republican Party, including the "President's Senior Political Advisor." This delegation sought to remind Rich that the Texas State Senate acted well within their rights and that what Dewhurst was suggesting was inconsistent with the historical procedure of the Texas Senate.[38] Days before the State of Texas quietly made its August 15 submission of a preclearance request, a Department of Justice spokesperson (Jorge Martinez) said the following: "This (two-thirds practice) is not a matter that we would need to look at under Section 5 of the Voting Rights Act. These are internal rules of the state Senate and, in our opinion would not be anything that we would have to look at."[39]

A few days before this incident, Van de Putte and the ten other senators filed a lawsuit in Travis County District Court. The lawsuit argued that under a prior case, *Balderas*, that was affirmed by the Supreme Court in 2002, the Texas congressional redistricting plan was valid for the rest of this decade until release of the next federal decennial census. In the *Balderas* case, the U.S. District Court for the Eastern District of Texas ordered a congressional redistricting plan into effect, determining in the process that its redistricting plan satisfied the one person-one vote requirement of the Equal Protection Clause of the United States. The State of Texas did not appeal the decision of this three-judge panel. Moreover, the lawsuit also argued against the lieutenant governor's "full constitutional authority" to compel attendance of absent members. Dewhurst claimed that he had, as sergeant-at-arms, "full legal authority" to arrest the absent members "wherever they may be found" in order to compel their attendance; he viewed it permissible to employ off-duty police officers, among others (rumors surfaced that bounty hunters were an option), to accomplish such arrests. The attorney for the eleven senators argued that Dewhurst's authorization violated Article III, section 14 of the Texas Constitution.[40] The lawsuit sought to protect the Texas Eleven from arrest.[41] In response to rumors about the possible arrest of the Texas Eleven, New Mexico Governor Bill Richardson vowed that the state police would arrest and charge with attempted kidnapping anyone who tried to remove the Senate refugees. New Mexico Republicans were criticizing Richardson over the cost of the security detail. Richardson tried to downplay the issue by saying it was a routine measure for visiting VIPs. No overtime funds were allocated for the half dozen officers on duty.[42] This issue never caught fire in the media.

Twenty-six days into the standoff, Van de Putte addressed some questions that had been brewing among media. The questions focused on the "process" and the "end game," and she replied by parodying the popular Mastercard commercial:

> If you must keep score, here it is in terms of money alone:
> On Special Sessions Misplaced Priorities:
> $3.4 million so far for a Republican redistricting power grab,
> Nothing for Texas school children and property taxpayers.
> On Redistricting Lawsuits:
> $5 million for a Republican redistricting power grab,
> Nothing for children's health care.
> On Changing the Congressional Primary Dates:
> $16 million to conduct a separate congressional primary in every district,
> Nothing for elderly care.
> On Placing a Price on Democracy:
> $627,000 in potential "Poll Tax" fines levied against eleven senators,
> Nothing to allow us to represent our minority constituents.
> Taking a stand for our priorities and democratic principles: priceless.[43]

On September 20, utilizing a coast-to-coast platform given to her by the national Democratic Party, Van de Putte delivered the Democratic response to President George Bush's weekly radio address. She began by saying: "When George W. Bush was our governor, we worked across party lines to address the challenges facing the people of Texas. Today, the United States faces many challenges: an education system that leaves millions of children behind, a health care system that leaves millions of families uninsured or without care, an economy that has left millions of Americans without jobs. But instead of working to solve these problems, the Republican majority has adopted a new playbook, the three Rs—recount, recall and re-redistricting—in an attempt to use government to expand partisan power."[44] The reality was that Van de Putte was uncertain about how this would all end. She had not planned an exit strategy and would let the courts decide what it would be.

Public Opinion

Since the summer of 2001, Montgomery and Associates, an independent research firm based in Austin, Texas, had been running surveys tracking statewide political issues and elected officials. In 2003, they conducted a survey that took place from July 2 to 16 and tested 1,031 Texas residents over the age of eighteen. This survey was a random sample of adult Texas residents matching the state's demographics. On the governor's job performance rating the numbers translate to a 45.5 percent positive and 48.6 percent negative rating. Except for a bump among Republicans (64.4 percent positive), Perry did not do particularly well among any group. He did particularly poor among Hispanics (51 percent negative), African Americans (73.4 percent negative) and Democrats (68.4 percent negative).

Perry's impression numbers were mixed: 33.7 percent had a favorable impression of him, 24.6 percent had an unfavorable impression, and 38.7 percent were neutral. These numbers were consistent among most demographic groups, except for the expected shifts among self-identified Republicans (51.9 percent favorable, 10.4 percent unfavorable) and Democrats (15.8 percent favorable, 43.1 percent unfavorable).[45]

This survey revealed that the issue of redistricting, or at least the way it was being played out, was clearly an issue of partisan politics. Van de Putte and the other Texas Eleven were experiencing another kind of survey from the general public via email, fax, phone, and mail. At Van de Putte's San Antonio office, every so often her staff would receive "for" or "against" responses, mostly from people living outside of her district. People living outside of San Antonio responded with more "against her redistricting efforts" than those people living inside San Antonio. What mattered to Van de Putte was that she was winning the battle of public opinion in her own district.

On September 1, with the second special session over, the media became impatient with the Texas Eleven. They wanted to know what was next for the exiled senators. Stories began to surface about infighting and certain senators leaving for Labor Day and not returning to Albuquerque. One senator in particular, John Whitmire of Houston, was growing restless. There was speculation among the other senators that he was conversing on a daily basis with Dewhurst and providing him with a report of their plans. In one photo opportunity, Van de Putte drew a figurative line in the sand to keep Senator Whitmire inside the senators' out-of-state fortress. She stated, "We work on consensus, no matter what you've heard. Even Travis and Bowie had a big old fight at the Alamo."[46]

On September 2, State Senator Whitmire "broke ranks and returned to Houston."[47] Whitmire's exit provided the governor with the twenty-one senators needed for a quorum and a third special session. As Democratic Caucus Chair, Van de Putte made the decision to return with the other senators to Austin. Van de Putte's decision was to fight the penalties that were imposed upon them. Her strategy was to equate the $57,000 fine that each senator had to pay before they could exercise their duty to vote to the famous Southern poll tax. Van de Putte "kept a large photocopy of a 1949 Bexar County poll tax receipt" in the Democrat's out-of-state hotel headquarters. For Van de Putte, the $1.75 levy was a reminder of a time when her parents and grandparents were paying poll taxes, taking literacy tests, and generally fighting for their right to vote.[48]

On September 18, the Senate's ugly atmosphere darkened as Republicans suspended fines and placed their Democratic colleagues on probation through January 2005.[49] The once amicable relationship between senators was lost amidst the partisan rhetoric of redistricting. Van de Putte reported to the *San Antonio Express News* editorial board that a Republican senator privately told her in the members' lounge off the Senate floor on September 18 that "if Democratic senators newly returned from a New Mexico walkout acted 'like Mexicans, you will be treated like Mexicans.'"[50] Van de Putte shared the comment with the *Express News* to illustrate the racial issues simmering in the months-long fight over redrawing Texas congressional districts. She refused to identify the Republican senator or four other Republican senators she said were also present, claiming that would violate a tradition of confidentiality covering talks in the lounge off the Senate floor.[51] The media, particularly the *San Antonio Express News*, mercilessly demanded that Van de Putte identify the Republican senator that she said had slurred Mexican Americans, but she remained steadfast to Senate confidentiality despite the negative image she endured. The media began to question the validity of her story and her credibility.[52]

By October 10, Van de Putte was under tremendous pressure to identify the Republican who uttered the slur. Every Republican state senator signed a letter addressing it to Van de Putte urging her to either name the GOP colleague or to withdraw her account of the comment. The letter stated that the GOP senators "fully support" lifting the confidentiality of the conversation "given that if indeed the incident took place, the Senatorial courtesy has already been violated."[53] Two days later, under pressure, Van de Putte retracted her charge that a Republican colleague privately slurred Mexicans. She said "I have nothing but respect for the men and women of the Texas Senate, Republicans and Democrats alike. And I am withdrawing any statements about comments in the members' lounge. . . . Apology was made. Apology accepted. It's a closed matter."[54] In the following weeks, the *San Antonio Express News* continued this debate in hopes of pressuring Van de Putte to reveal who had uttered those words, but it went nowhere. The public was tired of the issue and wanted to put the bickering behind them.

Between the stress of being in Albuquerque and the alleged racial slur by a Republican senator, Van de Putte's health was strained. She was struggling with a personal health scare. She had been feeling ill when she led the Texas Eleven to Albuquerque but could not find the time for a physical examination. While in Albuquerque she thought she was just exhausted because of the stress. When she returned to

Austin and met with her doctor, however, she was diagnosed with a thyroid condition common in women thirty to fifty years of age (an autoimmune disorder related to Hashimoto's disease). She began treatment for "abnormal cells" or dysplasia.[55] Rumors began to surface in the political community that Van de Putte would not be running for re-election in 2004. She quickly released a press statement reassuring her supporters that she did plan to seek re-election.

Summary

The ramifications of challenging the redistricting efforts by Republicans go beyond the examination of the political moment discussed in this chapter. The issue of race illuminates the racial, social, and political stakes in redistricting. This chapter suggests that race does matter in American politics, particularly in Texas. The political fight between the Texas Eleven and the Republicans begs us to consider the implications of "racially polarized voting." This concept suggests that whites and minorities will not vote for the same candidates. Moreover, the standoff also suggests that there are limitations to relying on biracial or multiracial coalitions of voters or legislators to advance Latino representation. The most interesting player in this struggle was Van De Putte, a Latina who challenged a traditional southern political culture that was interested in maintaining elite political participation.

Van de Putte's leadership was calculating and unwavering throughout the redistricting challenge. She had become a strategic politician. She knew that the struggle against redistricting had to occur on two fronts: in the media and through the courts. Her leadership was inclusive and decisive. Tony Proffitt, an Austin political consultant who worked for the late Democratic lieutenant governor Bob Bullock, agreed that Van de Putte proved herself over time. "She has become a leader in the state of Texas," he said. "She comes with a lot of experience and a lot of seniority and has the ability to get things done." As head of the Senate Democratic Caucus, she helped guide Senate Democrats into breaking a quorum needed to vote on a congressional redistricting plan, thereby temporarily halting a Republican effort.[56] Her leadership role in the Texas legislature propelled her to leadership positions at the national level. In December 2003, Van de Putte was elected President of the National Hispanic Caucus of State Legislators (NHCSL), a position she retained until 2005. The NHCSL's mission is to be the foremost organization serving and representing the interests of Hispanic state legislators from all states, commonwealths, and territories of the United States. In August 2005, Van de Putte was named president-elect of the prestigious National Conference of State Legislators (NCSL). She was the first Hispanic and the first Texan ever named president-elect of the organization and assumed the presidency from 2006 to 2007. NCSL is an effective and respected advocate for the interests of state governments before Congress and federal agencies and provides research, technical assistance, and opportunities for policymakers to exchange ideas on the most pressing state issues.

SEVEN

Looking Forward

THE FOCUS OF THIS BOOK is to further our understanding of the political behavior of Latinas as políticas in state politics using one case study. The states are important arenas of policymaking because they are the training grounds for higher office. My study contextualizes the experience of a Latina in the Texas state legislature. Van de Putte provides a rich case study of how Latinas can achieve positions of political prominence and why this hard-won prominence has significant repercussions.

My study contributes to research in the field of Latino politics by providing an in-depth analysis of a highly male-centered process. I show how a little girl from the west side of San Antonio became one of the most powerful Latinas in state politics and I raise questions about the way gender influences the process, including: Can women succeed on their own terms? Are they simply women playing a man's game according to men's rules and objectives or are they politicians who are reshaping the game? Is Van de Putte representative of a new generation of Latina politicians who have gone beyond being mere tokens? Answers to these questions will require further research. However, answering these questions in the context of Van de Putte's experiences will provide insight into how she fared and whether she has made a significant difference from a gender perspective.

Van de Putte moved steadily up the legislative ladder following her election to the House in 1991. She honed a reputation as a skilled negotiator, determined consensus builder, and "the hardest working member of the House."[1] Her approach is consistent with the literature about women in politics. For example, Jewell and Whicker found that women leaders were more likely than men to adopt a "consensus" style and much less likely to adopt a "command" style.[2] Similarly, Rosenthal reported that by large majorities, women legislators in 2004 said they not only do more independent research and study legislation in greater detail but also spend more time building consensus and seeking out all points of view than men do.[3] Over the years, Van de Putte has chaired a variety of committees and subcommittees, has been tapped by previous Speakers to serve on committees to keep members communicating about the issue, and has won her caucus's nomination as Speaker Designate.

I began this book by suggesting that as a Latina state legislator, Leticia Van de Putte represents a new generation of leaders that has reshaped the political culture in Texas. She managed to win re-election six times, positioned herself on critical committees that benefit the city of San Antonio directly, pushed key legislation through the state legislature, forced the Senate into a standstill during the 2003 redistricting effort of the Republican Party, and positioned herself to assume positions of national influence. She is only the second Latina to serve in the Texas Senate. Van de Putte represents a breakthrough in the Latina community's quest for political representation and status in Texas politics. Latinas are no longer viewed as meek and politically inexperienced. The importance of electing more Latinas to public office grows out of a belief that representative democracy demands that all citizens, regardless of gender and ethnicity, have an equal opportunity to participate in politics. Women's rights activists claim that positions of power are a matter of justice and equity. Furthermore, Latina politicians serve as role models for future generations of Latinas by encouraging them to overcome traditional cultural sex roles. For these symbolic reasons, then, the numerical presence of Latinas in the corridors of power is important. This study is important for those very reasons.

I now take a closer look at how Van de Putte was able to assume positions of power and what the conditions or pathways were for her to become the first Latina president of the National Conference of State Legislators. One reason Van de Putte represents a new generation of leaders is that she did not follow the traditional path of a Latina. According to Van de Putte, the first generation of Latinas worked as social workers, teachers, nurses, and secretaries. The second generation broke away from these traditional occupations and became pharmacists, lawyers, accountants, and so on. When Latinas are placed on committees, they get pigeonholed into those that serve first-generation occupations such as education and health. Van de Putte's committee assignments, however, have extended beyond education and health to business, commerce, and veteran and military affairs. As a pharmacist, Van de Putte represented the new generation of Latina politicians that refused to be anchored to the education and health committees. She pushed through major business bills, like the telecom bill, from which Latina legislators typically shy away.

I began this study by providing a purview of the obstacles to electing women to various offices. We know that a state's political culture, institutional behavior, political parties, and electoral opportunities can serve as obstacles to the electability of women. In the second chapter, I provided a purview of the literature on women, particularly Latinas, in politics. If we begin where all political scientists begin when trying to understand political behavior—with political socialization—we learn that individuals who were socialized in political households and who do not have to reconcile family life and public life have a less complex calculus to face when considering whether to enter politics.[4] In the San Miguel household, politics was always a topic of discussion. Van de Putte's godfather, former state senator Joe Bernal, was always running for some office and the San Miguel front yard always exhibited a political poster identifying their political support. As Van de Putte matured and entered college, she was more conscious of political issues but too busy with school and work to become involved. Her political maturation did not come to fruition until she married Pete Van de Putte. With a new husband and a growing family, she never involved herself in the party structure. She fulfilled the expected role of a Latina in the Democratic Party—she was a soldier who block walked with her children in tow, hosted tea parties, helped with fundraisers, and helped with campaign organizing. When she decided to run for office, she was not recruited or embraced by the Democratic Party structure; instead she developed her own network of support through her various professional associations and community involvement. It could be argued that her "go-it-alone" attitude benefited her greatly because she gained the support and confidence of a political machine, Los Tres Panchos (The Three Panchos), that did more for her than the Democratic Party. She was mentored by the politically powerful Frank Tejeda, who ran San Antonio's southside politics. He was a constant reminder that personalismo, the building of relationships with the constituents, was important for any state legislator.

Under Tejeda's auspices, Van de Putte learned how to work the legislature. She knew that if she wanted to be viewed as a leader, she would have to involve herself in the institutional party structure. She ran for various positions in party caucuses and organizations. The most valuable lesson she learned from Tejeda was that a connection to the people was important if one desired their political support. Looking back at her record as a legislator, one quickly surmises that she understood that personal connections with constituents are as important as developing relationships with her colleagues. In other words, for a Latina trying to survive in a good ol' boy's institution, symbolic policymaking is just as important as substantive policymaking.

After five years of experience, Van de Putte was presented with a political opportunity to elevate her political stature. The state Senate seat in her district was being vacated by the long-time San Antonio politico Gregory Luna. This is the same seat she considered running for after her first term in office. For medical reasons, she declined to challenge Luna for the seat. Others believed she withdrew out of respect for the time he had already put in as a state representative. By respectfully waiting her turn, the seat would be hers to win once he decided to surrender it.

Van de Putte did not take the decision to run for the State Senate lightly. She was rational and calculating in her thoughts. She had just passed major legislation that won her the support of the business interests, she was willing to work across party lines for public policy, and her communication skills gave her the influence to forge unlikely relationships. In her eyes, she had enough experience to win the seat and it was time to move on and face new challenges. In mid-1999, she announced that she planned to run for Luna's Senate seat in a special election. She beat most of her challengers for the party nomination except one, State Representative Leo Alvarado. He later dropped out of the two-way race because of his respect for Van de Putte.

If we look back at Van de Putte's list of challengers for state representative and state senator, the political opportunity was there for her to win. The only serious challenger she faced was David Leibowitz in 2000, who was the Republican challenger for Luna's seat, and he was a real threat because he had deep pockets. However, even deep pockets could not defeat Van de Putte, who beat Leibowitz 54.36 percent to 45.63 percent.

By the time Van de Putte reached the state Senate, she was a seasoned campaigner and politician. Nothing, however, could have prepared her for what she faced in the legislative session of 2003: redistricting. After one term she was made chair of the Democratic Caucus. Her Senate colleagues needed someone who would not waver under political pressure. "Van de Putte has the capability as a leader to draw you into her vision and make it seem as if it was your original idea."[5] The Albuquerque protest showcased her steady leadership skills and propelled her into the national spotlight. After her return from Albuquerque, she was elected president of the National Hispanic Caucus of State Legislators, a position she filled until 2005. In late 2005, Van de Putte was elected 2006–2007 president of the National Conference of State Legislatures (NCSL). The NCSL executive director, William Pound, said, "Senator Van de Putte has proven herself an effective leader within the Texas Senate and within the National Conference of State Legislatures. We are pleased to be able to tap her leadership skills as a resource for state legislatures from around the country."[6]

In many ways, Van de Putte's leadership is telling of what is to come as the state's demographics change. As second, third, and later generations of Latinas come of age and more opportunities become available to them, they will pursue nontraditional occupations. They will insist on being placed on committees that address nontraditional needs—like the Business and Commerce Committee—and that do not necessarily fit stereotypical expectations. Van de Putte has demonstrated that party support, at least for Latina women, is not as important as professional and personal networks, which provided her base of support. Furthermore, Texas's political culture is not going to change and diversity will always be an issue in the state legislature. Although Latina legislators may not control the legislature, Van de Putte's experience suggests that they can have influence and clout.

Why should we care about Latina legislative leadership? Democratic theory emphasizes the values of equality and representation in policymaking institutions. Mansbridge argues that new thinking about representation emphasizes the contributions of women to the quality of legislative deliberations, voter accountability, and constituent-legislator communication.[7] Having women in legislative leadership not only fulfills the democratic ideal of equality and representation but also translates into tangible benefits for women legislators. Having a Latina buck the traditional political culture of the history of redistricting in Texas suggests equality of influence.

As the presence of Latinas in the state legislatures has grown over the years, so has their share of leadership positions. Scholars have begun to explore the impact of gender, race, and ethnicity on the legislative products and the representational style of elected officials at the state level. Empirical investigations of how elected officials represent their constituents support the claim that social backgrounds matter and have a profound impact on political leadership, public policies, and legislative priorities. The mere symbol of a socially diverse elected government has political consequences well beyond the realm of public policy. Diversity in the legislature, then, can have a profound impact.

Given that only nine Latinas are in the Texas state legislature, measuring their collective impact is methodologically problematic. However, Hawkesworth contends that the mere presence of women of color in the legislature is transforming the institution, as they battle stereotypes of minority women and shape the public policy debate on issues pertaining to women and minority groups. In this way, one can theorize that they have an indelible effect (via influence) that cannot be washed away. Van de Putte's legacy is similar to former governor Ann Richard's legacy—show them you can be a strong leader with a feminine touch. While in the Texas legislature Van de Putte has challenged traditional political culture by demanding to be referred to as "Mrs.," indicating her married status, rather than "Ms.," as is customary; her serving as chair of the Democratic Caucus and leading the Texas 11 to Albuquerque, New Mexico, to protest redistricting (and bringing the Texas legislature to a standstill); and becoming the first Latina to serve as president of the NCSL.

What is next for Van de Putte's political future? She contends that she has no aspirations to run for any statewide office or to go to Washington, D.C. For her, the real power in policymaking, with tangible results, lies in the state. States can redraw districts or make districts disappear, thereby making U.S. Congressional seats disappear. She has this power. In addition, serving on the state legislature, which is a part-time legislature, gives her time to do other things in her life. She can still be a pharmacist. She can spend time with her family. She also stays more connected with the community. She enjoys her current position, and it is a place where much can be accomplished. For Van de Putte, the politics of Texas are never dull.

To conclude, I address the series of questions about the gendered process posed at the beginning of this chapter: Can women succeed on their own terms? Are they simply women playing a man's game according to men's rules and objectives, or are they reshaping the game? Does Van de Putte represent a new generation of Latina politicians who have gone beyond being mere tokens? First, Van de

Putte did partly succeed on her own terms. She was neither recruited by the Democratic Party nor embraced by party officials. She was, however, supported by individuals who belonged to the party. She was able to succeed on her own terms because of people like Frank Tejeda, Joe Bernal, and Paul Elizondo. Tejeda taught her how to survive politically and the importance of linking politics to policymaking. Latina politicians tend to focus more on policymaking and forget that politics are intimately linked to it.

As I observe Latina political participation in San Antonio, it can be argued that Van de Putte has become the Tejeda of her time minus the political machine. But she is not alone. Van de Putte (and Maria Antonietta Berriozábal) is the go-to person for endorsements of other Latinas who seek elected office. She acts as a mentor to them, explaining the ins and outs of politics. She provides them with a key piece of advice that has served her well, that is, convincing the voters that you (a Latina) can lead and be feminine enough to put them at ease about placing you in a position of power. She emphasizes the connection between politics and policy, a paradigm that men understand all too well. Most importantly, she exemplifies the idea that Latinas who want to assume elected office no long have to seek the approval or endorsement of Latino politicians. They can succeed on their own with their own gendered support networks if they understand the rules of the (political) game.

Second, Van de Putte and her Latina colleagues understand the masculine nature of the Texas legislature. The state's political culture is not friendly toward the election of women, much less Latina women. However, Van de Putte and her Latina colleagues are reshaping the game by the mere fact that they are present in that institution. Being the first Latina in the history of Texas to challenge the legislature by breaking a quorum, forcing it into a standstill, and leading eleven Democratic colleagues out of the state in protest is indicative of a politician who is reshaping the game. It is indicative of Latinas possessing the political power to influence political outcomes.

Third, Van de Putte does represent a new generation of Latina leaders. She, along with the other eight Latinas in the legislature, have nontraditional occupations. Women who are in nontraditional occupations tend to challenge traditional stereotypes. Moreover, Van de Putte exemplifies what Fraga and others call strategic intersectionality.[8] They argue that Latina legislators are effective advocates for working-class communities because they are uniquely positioned to leverage the intersectionality of their ethnicity and gender in ways that are of strategic benefit in the legislative process. These scholars contend that as ethnic women, their multiple identities better position them to build cross-group coalitions. As women, they have more opportunities to "soften" their ethnicity by posturing themselves as women, mothers, and community advocates. This makes them gender inclusive. Finally, they contend that as women, Latina legislators have a propensity to be more focused on the substance of policy of particular interest to working-class communities. The issues that are of greatest interest to them are education, health care, and jobs.

Van de Putte uses her multiple identities. She knows when to emphasize motherly concerns (such as children's health insurance), when to be a party player (like by leading the Democratic caucus), when to emphasize her ethnicity as a Latina legislator concerned about representation of minority groups (in issues such as redistricting), and when to emphasize her role as a female legislator (for example, on the patients' bill of rights and through mentorship). She is aware of her unique communication skills, collective decision making, and ability to forge cross-party coalitions to pass major legislation. Van de Putte exemplifies a strategic politician, which is what the next generation of Latina leaders must also strive for.

APPENDIX ONE: WOMEN IN THE TEXAS STATE LEGISLATURE, 1991–2005

	1991	1993	1995	1997	1999	2001	2003	2005
HOUSE								
Hispanic women	4	8	8	8	7	6	7	7
Non-Hispanic women	14	16	21	21	22	24	25	24
All Hispanics, men and women	18	24	26	28	28	27	30	29
All women, all races	18	24	29	29	29	30	32	31
SENATE								
Hispanic women	1	1	1	1	2	2	2	2
Non-Hispanic women	3	3	3	3	1	2	2	2
All Hispanics, men and women	5	6	7	7	7	7	7	7
All women, all races	4	4	4	4	3	4	4	4

APPENDIX TWO: LEGISLATIVE RECORD OF HISPANIC WOMEN SERVING IN THE TEXAS LEGISLATURE

Source of chart data: Texas legislature at http://www.capitol.state.tx.us.

(Chart begins on next page)

Legend

HB	House Bill
HCR	House Concurrent Resolution
HJR	House Joint Resolution
HR	House Resolution
HCM	House Congratulatory Motion
HMM	House Memorial Motion
SB	Senate Bill
SCR	Senate Concurrent Resolution
SJR	Senate Joint Resolution
SR	Senate Resolution

		LEGISLATIVE SESSION								
		72nd	73rd	74th	75th	76th	77th	78th	79th	80th
Christina Hernandez	HB	14	23	20	18					
	HCR	–	1	1	1					
	HJR	1	1	1	1					
	HR	8	4	5	6					
	SB	–	3	2	4					
	SCR	–	–	1	1					
	SR	–	1	–	–					
Diana Davila	HB		13	15	30					
	HCR		2	2	2					
	HR		5	15	7					
	SB		1	–	6					
	SCR		–	1	–					
Elvira Reyna	HB			11	11	8				
	HCR			–	–	2				
	HR			4	–	2				
	SB			3	5	1				
	SCR			–	2	–				
Irma Rangel	HB	14	12	24	23	29				
	HCR	1	–	1	1	2				
	HR	2	4	2	2	–				
	SB	2	7	4	10	10				
	SCR	2	–	2	2	–				
Yolanda Flores	HB		16							
	HJR		1							
	HR		3							
	HCM		102							
	HMM		2							

		LEGISLATIVE SESSION								
		72nd	73rd	74th	75th	76th	77th	78th	79th	80th
Judith Zaffirini	HB						38	21	37	46
	HCR						5	1	4	3
	HJR						1	–	–	1
	SB						72	102	71	84
	SCR						2	2	1	1
	SJR						2	–	–	1
	SR						24	41	42	44
Leticia	HB	3	23	45	57	50	59	27	30	36
Van de Putte	HCR	–	1	1	4	3	1	7	2	6
	HJR	–	–	1	1	–	1	–	3	–
	HR	5	4	12	14	12	–	–	–	–
	SB	–	4	16	23	18	86	85	97	110
	SCR	–	1	1	3	1	2	1	–	4
	SR	–	–	–	–	–	29	53	43	72
	SJR	–	–	–	–	1	–	3	1	2
Sylvia Romo	HB		23	56						
	HCR		–	1						
	HJR		2	4						
	HR		1	3						
	SB		4	3						
	SJR		2	–						
Vilma Luna	HB		–	17	28	35				
	HCM		1	–	–	–				
	HCR		1	2	–	2				
	HJR		–	–	–	1				
	HR		–	6	9	6				
	SB		–	4	1	5				
	SCR		–	1	–	–				

NOTES

INTRODUCTION

1. Consistent with the convention used in Hardy-Fanta's *Latina Politics, Latino Politics* and Sonia Garcia and others' *Políticas*, the terms "Latina," "Hispanic," "Mexican American," "Mexican," and "Chicana" will be used interchangeably in the present work.

2. Navarro, "Latina Mayors," which includes an interview with Blanca Sanchez Vela.

3. Lisa Marie Gomez, "Border City Elects Woman," *San Antonio Express News*, May 3, 1999: 1A.

4. Sonia Garcia conducted an interview with Elizabeth "Betty" Flores on January 8, 2004. This excerpt appears in my chapter, "Latina Mayors," 97.

5. Gary Scharrer and Peggy Fikac, "High Court Targets South Texas District," *San Antonio Express News*, June 29, 2006: 1A.

6. Hardy-Fanta, *Latina Politics, Latino Politics*.

CHAPTER ONE

1. Seligman, Kink, and Kim, *Patterns of Recruitment*, 160.

2. Susan Welch, "Recruitment of Women to Public Office," *Western Political Quarterly* 31 (September 1978): 372–80.

3. Barrett, "Black Women in State Legislatures,"; Moncrief, Thompson. and Schuhmann, "Gender, Race, and the State Legislature"; Fraga et al., "Strategic Intersectionality."

4. Cohen, "Portrait of Marginality"; Montoya, Hardy-Fanta, and Garcia, "Latina Politics."

5. Dolan, *Voting for Women*.

6. Elazar, *American Federalism*, 85.

7. Kirkpatrick, *Political Woman*; Kelly and Boutilier, *Making of Political Women*.

8. Kirkpatrick, *Political Woman,* 14.

9. The slogan can be found at Office of Governor Economic Development and Tourism http://www.governor.state.tx.us/ecodev/.

10. Daniel Elazar's 1972 study *American Federalism* puts states into three categories of political culture—Moralistic, Individualistic, or Traditionalistic—with some states categorized as a mixture of two. Moralistic states place primary value on "politics as a public activity centered on some notion of the public good and properly devoted to the advancement of the public interest" (90). Individualistic states are defined as those that "emphasize the centrality of private concerns, (and) it places a premium on limiting community intervention . . . into private activities" (86–87). Traditionalistic states have an electorate "that accepts a substantially hierarchical society as part of the ordered nature of things . . . (and that) tries to limit (the role of government) to securing the continued maintenance of the existing social order" (93).

11. Hill, "Political Culture."

12. Rule, "Electoral Systems."

13. Maxwell and Crain, *Texas Politics Today.*

14. Ibid.

15. Speech by Sylvia Rodriguez to the Robert A. Taft Institute of Government. She was elected to participate in the Democratic National Committee on July 18, 1978. Her speech was titled "Changing Political Parties: The Impact on Executives and Legislatures" (unpublished), and in it she reminded her listeners of the changes brought about by the McGovern Rules.

16. State Representative Paul Moreno, unpublished memo from Law Offices of Moreno & Briones, Attorneys at Law, 1140 Southwest National Bank Bldg., El Paso, Tex. 79901, September 27, 1974.

17. Rosales, *The Illusion of Inclusion.*

18. Cynthia Orozco, "Mexican American Democrats," *Handbook of Texas Online,* http://www.tsha.utexas.edu/handbook/online/articles/MM/wmm2.html (accessed July 5, 2006).

19. Freeman, "Political Culture."

20. Leticia Van de Putte, in interview with author, July 6, 2006.

21. Freeman, *Room at a Time;* Fowlkes, Perkins, and Tolleson-Rinehart, "Gender Roles."

22. Clift and Brazaitis, in *Madam President,* write about the reluctance of former Senator Bob Dole to publicly endorse his wife, Elizabeth Dole's, presidential campaign in 2000. They write, "Dole also confided that he was thinking of contributing money to a rival candidate, John McCain, a colleague from the Senate" (93). In addition, because of the lack of financial support given to women candidates, the authors also discuss the creation of Emily's

List and WISH List. Both organizations were created by women to provide financial support specifically for female candidates.

23. Carroll, *Women as Candidates;* Wilma Rule, "Why Women Don't Run: The Critical Contextual Factors in Women's Legislative Recruitment," *Western Political Quarterly* 43, no.2 (1981): 437–48.

24. Sonia Garcia, "Texas Women"; Sonia Garcia et al., *Políticas;* Potter, "Women in the Texas Legislature"; Jones and Winegarten, *Capitol Women.*

25. Boles, "Texas Women in Politics."

26. Tolleson-Rinehart and Stanley, *Claytie and the Lady.*

27. Stanley, "Gender Politics in the 1994 Texas Election."

28. Maxwell and Crain, *Texas Politics Today.*

29. According to the Texas Legislative Reference Library, the 78th 2003 legislative session was the last session to include an ethnic breakdown of its members. An informal count of the number of African Americans in the 79th 2005 legislature reveals 12 African Americans (six men and six women) in the state House of Representatives and two African American males in the state Senate. For more information see http://www.lrl.state.tx.us/legis/leaders/lrlhome.

30. In the midterm elections of 2006, State Representative Martha Wong would lose her re-election bid to her Democratic challenger, an Anglo female.

31. These numbers come from the Center for American Women and Politics at the Eagleton Institute of Politics at Rutgers University. The information cited can be found at the following address: www.cawp.rutgers.edu/Facts/StbySt/Tex.

32. National Directory of Latino Elected Officials 2005.

33. Ibid.

34. Rule and Norris, "Anglo and Minority"; Welch and Herrick, "Impact of At-Large Elections."

35. Montoya el al., "Latina Politics"; Luis Ricardo Fraga et al., "Gender and Ethnicity"; Tate, "Women and State Legislatures."

36. *Women of Color in Elective Office,* 2007, Rutgers University, Center for American Women and Politics, Eagleton Institute of Politics, at www.cawp.rutgers.edu.

37. *Elección Latina-State Legislators,* 2007, Rutgers University, Center for American Women and Politics, Eagleton Institute of Politics, at http://www.cawp.rutgers.edu/Eleccion/elecleg.htm.

38. Seidman, *Interviewing and Qualitative Research,* 4.

39. Strauss and Corbin, *Basics of Qualitative Research,* 12.

40. Ibid.

41. Luis Ricardo Fraga et al., "Gender and Ethnicity."

42. Hill, "Political Culture."

43. This term was used by Bedolla, Tate, and Wong in "Indelible Effects."

CHAPTER TWO

1. Darcy, Welch, and Clark, *Women, Elections, and Representation;* Burrell, "Women Candidates."

2. Darcy, Welch, and Clark, *Women, Elections, and Representation,* and Burrell, "Women Candidates"; Matland and King, "Sex and the Grand Old Party."

3. Jacobson, "Strategic Politicians"; Gertzog, "Women's Changing Pathways"; Luis Fraga et al., "Strategic Intersectionality."

4. Hardy-Fanta, "Latina Women and Political Consciousness," 224.

5. Chispa: a gleam or spark that passes quickly.

6. Baca Zinn, "Gender and Ethnicity."

7. Sapiro and Farah, "New Pride & Old Prejudice."

8. Bledsoe and Herring, "Victims of Circumstances"; Sapiro, *Political Integration of Women.*

9. Hardy-Fanta, "Latina Women and Political Consciousness," 233.

10. Enloe, *Curious Feminist.*

11. Fowlkes, "Ambitious Political Women."

12. Carroll, *Women as Candidates;* Darcy, Welch, and Clark, Women, Elections and Representation.

13. Gaddie and Bullock, "Structural and Elite Features."

14. Schlesinger, *Ambition and Politics;* Carroll, *Women as Candidates;* Norris and Lovenduski, *Political Recruitment;* Welch and Studlar, "Multimember Districts."

15. Norris, "Impact of the Electoral System."

16. Thomas and Wilcox, *Women and Elective Office.*

17. Ibid., 4.

18. "Eligibility pool" appears in Thomas and Wilcox, *Women and Elective Office,* 94; Sonia Garcia and Marisela Marquez, "Mobilizing Change: An Examination of Latina Political Organizations" (paper presented at the annual conference for the Western Political Science Association, Oakland, Calif., March 16–18, 2005.

19. Jacobson, "Strategic Politicians"; Gertzog, "Women's Changing Pathways."

20. Luis Fraga et al., "Strategic Intersectionality: Gender, Ethnicity, and Political Incorporation," Paper prepared for the Annual Meeting of the American Political Science Association, Washington, D.C., August 31–September 4, 2005.

21. Melville, *Twice a Minority.*

22. Montoya, Hardy-Fanta, and Garcia, "Latina Politics."

23. Takash, "Breaking Barriers to Representation."

24. Garcia and Marquez, "Motivational and Attitudinal Factors," 111.

25. Hardy-Fanta, *Latina Politics, Latino Politics,* 25.

26. Pardo, "Mexican American Grassroots."

27. Takash, "Breaking Barriers to Representation," 419.

28. Gutierrez and Deen, *Chicanas in Texas Politics.*

29. Guerra, "Emergence of Ethnic Officeholders."

30. Jackson and Preston, *Racial and Ethnic Politics.*

31. Hardy-Fanta, *Latina Politics, Latino Politics.*

32. Brittney Booth, "Mayor Won't Seek Re-election," *Brownsville Herald,* May 21, 2003.

33. Garcia et al., *Políticas.*

34. Witt, Paget, and Matthews, *Running as a Woman,* 119.

35. Ibid., 118.

36. Gutierrez and Deen, *Chicanas in Texas Politics.*

37. Takash, "Breaking Barriers to Representation," 426.

38. Gutierrez and Deen, *Chicanas in Texas Politics.*

39. MacManus, "Voter Participation and Turnout."

40. Mansbridge, "Rethinking Representation."

41. Valian, *Why So Slow?*

42. Hochschild and Machung, *Second Shift.*

43. Jamieson, *Beyond the Double Bind.*

44. Gilligan, *In a Different Voice.*

45. Takash, "Breaking Barriers to Representation," 429.

46. Helgesen, *Female Advantage,* 21.

47. Eagly and Johnson, "Gender and Leadership Style."

48. Jewell and Whicker, *Legislative Leadership.*

49. Rosenthal, *When Women Lead.*

50. Rosenthal, "Gender Styles."

51. Chapman, "Presence, Promise, and Progress."

52. Mansbridge, "Should Blacks Represent Blacks."

53. Pitkin, *Concept of Representation.* According to Pitkin the idea of interests is necessary to the act of representing.

54. Carroll, "Representing Women."

55. Bratton and Haynie, "Agenda Setting."

56. Tamerius, "Sex, Gender, and Leadership."

57. Sinclair, "Distribution of Committee Positions," 285.

58. Hibbing, *Congressional Careers.*

59. Arnold and King, "Women, Committees, and Institutional Change."

60. Norton, "Women, It's Not Enough"; Dobson, "Representing Women's Interests."

61. Vega and Firestone, "Effects of Gender."

62. Bratton and Haynie, "Agenda Setting"; Thomas, "Impact of Women."

63. Duerst-Lahti, "Knowing Congress."

64. 110th Congress of the United States.

65. Mansbridge, "Should Blacks Represent Blacks"; Tamerius, "Sex, Gender, and Leadership."

CHAPTER THREE

1. Isabelle A. Ortiz, interviewed by author, October 5, 2005.

2. Ibid.

3. Leticia Van de Putte, interviewed by author, July 17, 2006.

4. City of San Antonio, "Market Square: A History,"

http://www.sanantonio.gov/sapar/marketsquarehistory (accessed May 4, 2005).

5. Ibid.

6. Ibid.

7. Pete Van de Putte, interviewed by author, December 9, 2003.

8. Daniel San Miguel, interviewed by author, January 8, 2004.

9. The word *curandero* comes from the Spanish word *curar,* which means to cure. Curanderos are people who practice folk medicine.

10. David Anthony Richelieu, "Toilet Training a Big City Issue," *San Antonio Express News,* July 31, 1991.

11. Paul Elizondo, interviewed by author, December 8, 2003.

12. After Leticia graduated as a pharmacist in 1979, she had her first child, Nicole, in May 1980, Vanessa in August 1981, Henry in October 1983, Gregory in November 1985, Isabella in July 1987, and Paul in July 1989.

13. Rosales, *The Illusion of Inclusion,* 65–66.

14. Dickens, "Political Role of Mexican Americans," 29.

15. Rosales, *The Illusion of Inclusion,* 81.

CHAPTER FOUR

1. Orozco, "Mexican American Democrats."

2. Private e-mail from Hector Hernandez, City Hall, San Antonio, July 20, 2006.

3. Rosales, *The Illusion of Inclusion,* 163.

4. *San Antonio Express News,* "Republican Texas House Candidate Bart Simpson Said He Would Bring," October 12, 1990.

5. Little, Dunn, and Deen, "View from the Top."

6. KLRN Public Television, "Polithon '90," Transcript, October 21, 1990.

7. Ibid.

8. Garcia et al., *Políticas.*

9. Rosales, *The Illusion of Inclusion,* 167.

10. *San Antonio Express News,* "Suggestions for the Election," October 11, 1990.

11. Ibid.

12. *San Antonio Express News,* "November Election Texas Representative Republican Bart Simpson Tried," November 7, 1990.

13. Rosales, *The Illusion of Inclusion,* 174.

14. *San Antonio Express News,* "The Bexar County Delegation to the Legislature Told City Council," November 16, 1990.

15. Diehl Kemper, "Texas Legislators are Facing Megaproblems in '91 Session," *San Antonio Express News,* December 16, 1990.

16. Ibid.

17. Leticia Van de Putte, interviewed by author, July 6, 2006.

18. Richard Smith, "Lawmaker Plans Sale to Avoid Conflict," *San Antonio Express News,* May 5, 1991.

19. "Find legs" is a term used among House members. It means that a member is going to take a walk and not be present in the chamber for the vote. The member will not vote "no," but just will not vote at all, which translates into a "yes" vote.

20. Bruce Davidson, "Redistricting Changes Dramatic for Bexar," *San Antonio Express News,* December 27, 1991.

21. Bruce Davidson, "Poor Treatment May Force Krier Out of Senate," *San Antonio Express News,* May 5, 1991.

22. Bruce Davidson, "Mayor Lilia Cockrell, Wins Handily," *San Antonio Express News,* December 9, 1991, and by same author, "Bexar Delegation Faces Big Changes: Eight of 14 Lawmakers May Shift," *San Antonio Express News,* July 7, 1991.

23. Bruce Davidson, "Races: Bexar Reps Eye District Changes," *San Antonio Express News,* January 5, 1992.

24. Bruce Davidson, "Filings: Bonilla Files for Bustamante's Seat," *San Antonio Express News,* January 2, 1991.

25. Bruce Davidson, "Bexar Delegation to Get Face Lift Number of Legislative Rookies Highlights Changes in Representation," *San Antonio Express News,* May 18, 1992.

26. J. Michael Parker and Don Driver, "Voters Guide Four State House Races Contested in Bexar," *San Antonio Express News,* October 14, 1992.

27. Ibid.

28. Edna McGaffey, "Outstanding Women in 1991 Artist Given Lifetime Achievement Recognition," *San Antonio Express News,* March 22, 1992.

29. Don Finley, "Dermatologist Sounds Warning against Getting Too Much Sun," *San Antonio Express News*, April 2, 1992.

30. *San Antonio Express News*, "Briefcase: Architectural Firm Names Three," April 12, 1992.

31. Cindy Tumiel, "Teachers Union Grades Bexar's Lawmakers," *San Antonio Express News,* August 27, 1991.

32. Ibid.

33. Bruce Davidson, "Dutmer Gets Conservative Group's Nod," *San Antonio Express News,* October 20, 1992: 4A.

34. Marty Sabota, "Hospital Debate Doctors: Hospital's Plan Hurts Poor Kids," *San Antonio Express News,* June 23, 1992.

35. Stephanie Scott and Diana R. Fuentes, "Richards: Let Voters Decide School Finance," *San Antonio Express News,* November 11, 1992.

36. Stefanie Scott and Cindy Tumiel, "Lame-Duck Lawmakers Called Key to Approval of School Finance Bill," *San Antonio Express News,* November 10, 1992.

37. In 1987, Texas District Judge Harley Clark, in *Edgewood v. Kirby,* ruled that the state's system of financing its public schools violated its own constitution and laws. In October 1989, the Texas Supreme Court unanimously upheld Clark's ruling that the system was unconstitutional and gave the legislature until May 1, 1990, to fix it. In June 1990, the legislature passed, and the governor signed, a bill calling for somewhat increased funding to be phased in over a five-year period. In September 1990, Texas District Judge Scott McCown found the new law to be unconstitutional because it perpetuated the inequities of the old system. In January 1991, the Texas Supreme Court agreed with him, and the process went back to the drawing board.

38. Scott and Fuentes, "Richards: Let Voters Decide . . ."

39. Bruce Davidson, "Senate Race on Minds of Bexar Lawmakers," *San Antonio Express News,* December 12, 1998.

40. Adolfo Pesquera, "Gas Station Crime Dropping," *San Antonio Express News,* January 3, 1999.

41. Melissa Prentice, "San Antonio Fares Well at Close of Legislative Session," *San Antonio Express News,* June 1, 1999.

42. Sanford Nowlin, "Phone Firms Wage Bitter Ad War," *San Antonio Express News,* April 1, 1999.

43. Matt Flores, "Five Vie for Luna's Senate Post," *San Antonio Express News,* October 5, 1999.

44. *San Antonio Express News,* "Van de Putte Best Candidate for Senate," October 15, 1999.

45. Bruce Davidson, "Political Activist Turns Focus on Higher Ed," *San Antonio Express News,* October 23, 1999.

46. Matt Flores, "Van de Putte, Alvarado Likely Bound for Runoff," *San Antonio Express News,* November 3, 1999.

47. Matt Flores, "Alvarado Withdraws from State Senate Race," *San Antonio Express News,* November 4, 1999.

48. Jacque Crouse, "New Incumbent Faces Challenge," *San Antonio Express News,* February 28, 2000.

49. Sherry Sylvester, "Van de Putte, Leibowitz Vie for State Senate Seat," *San Antonio Express News,* March 11, 2000.

50. Nora Lopez, "Van de Putte Slightly Ahead of Leibowitz in District 26," *San Antonio Express News,* March 15, 2000.

CHAPTER FIVE

1. Stefanie Scott, "Our Rookie in County's Legislative Class of '92," *San Antonio Express News,* December 7, 1992.

2. In the Spanish language, *padrino* and *compadre* mean godfather and protector, respectively. *Padrino* refers to your godfather and *compadre* refers to your child's godfather.

3. Leticia Van De Putte, interviewed by author, July 6, 2006.

4. Rosales, *The Illusion of Inclusion,* 147.

5. The Official Leticia Van de Putte Campaign Site, "Meet State Senator Leticia Van de Putte," http://www.leticiavandeputte.com/meet.asp (accessed April 6, 2006).

6. The Council of State Governments: Eastern Regional Conference, "National Hispanic Caucus of State Legislators (NHCSL) Executive Committee Meeting and Business Board of Advisors Meeting," http://www.csgeast.org/page.asp?id=annmeetnhcsl (accessed May 20, 2006).

7. National Conference of State Legislatures, "Immediate Past President Senator Leticia Van de Putte, Texas," http://www.ncsl.org/programs/press/bio_vandeputte.htm (accessed June 3, 2006).

8. Smith and Deering, *Committees in Congress,* 18.

9. Sinclair, "Distribution of Committee Positions," 276.

10. Hibbing, *Congressional Careers.*

11. Rickey Dailey, "Laney to Decide Which Reps Get Power," *Valley Morning Star,* January 14, 2001.

12. Cox and McCubbins, *Legislative Leviathan,* 8.

13. Masters, "Committee Assignments," 345.

14. Ibid., 357.

15. Ibid., 356.

16. Dailey, "Laney to Decide"; Jerry Reed, "Taylor Redistricting Fight Begins," *Austin American Statesman,* January 5, 2001.

17. For example, Appropriations (members control the state budget),

Business and Industry (members are in charge of regulation of business and, for the past decade, probusiness legislation), Regulated Industry (members led the transition from high regulation to no regulation in critical industries such as energy), State Affairs (members deal with issues such as abortion and gay marriage), Civil Practices (members deal with issues related to tort reform and asbestos reform), Ways and Means (deals with any new taxes in the state), Education (critical to the state of Texas), and Criminal Justice. The critical committee for the House is the Calendar Committee, and the House Administration Committee is also important, particularly for staffers, because a tremendous number of rules exist that need to be followed by staffers.

18. Chapman, "Symbols and Substance."

19. Hero and Tolbert, "Latinos and Substantive Representation," 641.

20. Symbolic legislation means House or Senate resolutions, House or Senate concurrent resolutions, and House and Senate joint resolutions.

21. "Members and Leaders of the Texas State Legislature," http://www.lrl.state.tx.us/.

22. Ibid.

23. Morrow, *Republic If You Can.*

24. Chapman, "Symbols and Substance."

25. Few bills among the thousands that are introduced make it out of the state legislature and become public law. Thus, individual members are beating large odds if one of their bills becomes law. What types of bills become laws? While the public might imagine that in the competition of bills and resolutions only the most pressing and important public policies become a matter of state law, this is not always the case.

CHAPTER SIX

1. A quorum is the number of members required to conduct legislative business. Two-thirds of the elected members constitute a quorum in each house. A majority of the appointed members of a committee forms a quorum for the purpose of conducting committee business.

2. R.G. Ratcliffe and Rachel Graves, "Dewhurst Considers Legal Action Against Democrats," *Houston Chronicle,* August 6, 2003.

3. Terrence Stutz, "Senators Agree to Delay Action on Election Plan," *Dallas Morning News,* April 6, 1993.

4. Ciro Rodriguez, "Taking a Stand for Principle," *Immediate Press Release,* August 8, 2003.

5. Leticia Van de Putte, interviewed by author, October 5, 2006.

6. Ibid.

7. Ibid.

8. Ken Herman, "Perry Calls 2nd Special Session as 11 Escape to New Mexico," *Austin American Statesman,* July 29, 2003.

9. Ibid.

10. Kelly Shannon and Richard Benke, "Dems Flee to Protest Texas Redistricting," *Associated Press,* July 29, 2003.

11. Jim Forsyth, "Texas House Passes Redistricting Plan, Democrats Remain in New Mexico," *San Antonio Express News,* July 29, 2003.

12. Jon Sarche, "Colorado Court to Rule on Redistricting," *Fort-Worth Star-Telegram,* September 8, 2003.

13. Chuck Lindell, "Results of Remap Will Last Past '04: Decade-Long Control of U.S. House Could Rest on Texas Redistricting," *Austin American Statesman,* August 3, 2003.

14. Author interview with Leticia Van de Putte, July 17, 2006.

15. Ibid.

16. Gerry Herbert, "Memo: Strategy for Adjournment Sine Die," memorandum to Sen. Van de Putte and others, August 5, 2003 (unpublished).

17. Susan Hays, "Fund-raising Plan and Legal Parameters for Litigation Fund," memorandum to Sen. West, Rep. Dunnam, and Rep. Wolens, August 18, 2003.

18. State Senator Leticia Van de Putte, "Statement of the Texas 11," press release, August 25, 2003.

19. Jon Herskovitz, "Fugitive Texas Democrats Helped by Web Drive," *Reuters,* August 23, 2003; State Senator Leticia Van de Putte, "Statement of Senate Democrats in New Mexico," press release, September 3, 2003.

20. Fenton Communications, "Texas Senators to Barnstorm U.S.: Expose Bush Plan to Reduce Latino Voting Power," *Media Advisory,* September 4, 2003.

21. Shea Anderson, "Lone Star Politics Ambles to N.M.," *Albuquerque Tribune,* July 30, 2003.

22. Renee Montagne, "State Senator Leticia Van de Putte Discusses the Texas Democrats' Self-Imposed Exile in New Mexico," *National Public Radio,* August 22, 2003.

23. State Senator Leticia Van de Putte, "Update," press release, August 4, 2003.

24. Janet Elliott and Armando Villafranca, "Perry Hints at Another Session for Legislature," *Houston Chronicle,* August 1, 2003.

25. Peggy Fikac and Guillermo Garcia, "Perry Says Demos Put Funds at Risk," *San Antonio Express News,* August 1, 2003.

26. State Senator Leticia Van de Putte, "Another Day," press release, August 5, 2003.

27. W. Gardner Selby and Peggy Fikac, "New: GI Forum Says Perry Is Retaliating against Group's Redistricting Stand," *San Antonio Express News,* August 5, 2003.

28. Matt Angle, memo to Senator Royce West and Texas 11, August 4, 2003 (unpublished).

29. Leticia Van de Putte, personal correspondence with the author, August 4, 2003.

30. A robo call is a prerecorded telephone call—that is, a telephone call made using a computer that plays a voice recording, used in election campaigning and telemarketing.

31. Leticia Van de Putte, press release, August 13, 2003.

32. Leticia Van de Putte, "Statement of Senator Leticia Van de Putte," press release, August 18, 2003.

33. Patsy Spaw, "Penalties Imposed under Call of the Senate," memorandum to Lt. Gov. David Dewhurst, August 15, 2003.

34. Michael King, "Senators, Go to Your Rooms: First Fines, Then Probation, and Next—Detention and Curfew?" *Austin Chronicle,* September 26, 2003, http://www.austinchronicle.com. Accessed June 17, 2005.

35. April Castro, "Former Gov. Richards Blasts Perry for Redistricting Flap," *Associated Press,* August 11, 2003.

36. Guillermo X. Garcia, "Senators Might Go to Court," *San Antonio Express News,* August 1, 2003.

37. Leticia Van de Putte, "Statement of Members of the Texas 11," press release, August 20, 2003; Geoffrey S. Connor, Assistant Secretary of State, Applicability of Section 5 of Voting Right Act Letter, August 15, 2003 (unpublished memo to members of the Texas Eleven).

38. Letter from the Texas Congressional delegation to Section Chief Joseph Rich of the Voting Rights Section of the U.S. Department of Justice, August, 21, 2003.

39. Quoted in editorial, *El Paso Times,* August 12, 2003.

40. Article III (which covers the legislative department), section 14 (which covers privilege from arrest) states that senators and representatives shall, except in cases of treason, felony, or breach of the peace, be privileged from arrest during the session of the legislature, and in going to and returning from the same (amended November 1, 1999).

41. *Gonzalo Barrientos et al., v. State of Texas et al.,* 290 F. Supp.2d 740 (S.D. Tex. 2003).

42. Guillermo X. Garcia, "N.M. Cops Guard Texas Lawmakers," *San Antonio Express News,* July 30, 2003.

43. Leticia Van de Putte, "Statement of the Albuquerque Inmates . . . DRAFT," press release, August 22, 2003.

44. Leticia Van de Putte, "Democratic Response to the President's Weekly Radio Address," transcript of radio broadcast, September 20, 2003.

45. The margin of error was plus or minus 3.1 percent. For more information, see Jeff Montgomery, "Texans Opposed Redistricting: Governor's Approval Numbers Mediocre," press release, July 23, 2003.

46. R. G. Ratcliffe, "Texas 11 Face Hard Choices in Redistricting Flap," *Houston Chronicle,* September 1, 2003.

47. Melissa Drosjack and Armando Villafranca, "Bush Help Sought to End Remap War: Demos Take Case to Washington," *Houston Chronicle,* September 5, 2003.

48. Laylan Copelin, "Redistricting Hits Close to Home for 2 Lawmakers: Thoughts of Race, Repression Drive Van de Putte, Wentworth," *Austin American Statesman,* September 14, 2003.

49. R. G. Ratcliffe, "Texas Legislature Special Session: GOP Senators Put Texas 11 on Probation," *Houston Chronicle,* September 19, 2003.

50. Gardner W. Selby, "GOP Senators Are Demanding a Name; Some Are Skeptical that Van de Putte Heard Anyone Utter a Racial Slur," *San Antonio Express News,* October 9, 2003.

51. Gardner W. Selby, "Probe Eyed in Racial Allegation: Van de Putte Alleges Remark by a GOP Lawmaker," *San Antonio Express News,* October 8, 2003.

52. The lounge, a Senators-only room at the capitol where members mingle and fraternize out of the public eye, operates under a code of courtesy that basically says, "Whatever is said here, stays here." See Jaime Castillo, "Naming Names May Be Van de Putte's Only Way Out of Her Jam," *San Antonio Express News,* October 11, 2003 and "Our Turn: For Public, Controversy over Slur Hasn't Ended," *San Antonio Express News,* October 14, 2003.

53. Gardner W. Selby, "Remap Hits Another Snag; Meanwhile GOP Insists Van De Putte Put Up or Shut Up on Slur," *San Antonio Express News,* October 11, 2003.

54. Gardner W. Selby, "Senator Withdraws Allegation of Slur, Says She Received Colleague's Apology," *San Antonio Express News,* October 13, 2003.

55. Rebecca Rodriguez, "A Roller-Coaster Year," *San Antonio Express News,* November 16, 2003.

56. Ibid.

CHAPTER SEVEN

1. Eliot Shapliegh, interviewed by author, December 22, 2003.

2. Jewell and Whicker, *Legislative Leadership.*

3. Rosenthal, "Women Leading Legislature."

4. Lawless and Fox, *It Takes a Candidate,* 70.

5. Eliot Shapleigh, interviewed by author, December 22, 2003.

6. National Conference of State Legislatures, "Immediate Past President Senator Leticia Van de Putte, Texas," http://www.ncsl.org/programs/press/bio_vandeputte.htm (accessed June 3, 2006).

7. Mansbridge, "Rethinking Representation."

8. Fraga et al., "Strategic Intersectionality."

BIBLIOGRAPHY

Acker, Joan. "Hierarchies, Jobs, Bodies: A Theory of Gendered Organizations." *Gender and Society* 4, no. 2 (1990): 139–58.

Arnold, Laura W., and Barbara M. King. "Women, Committees, and Institutional Change in the Senate." In *Women Transforming Congress*, edited by Cindy Simon Rosenthal. Norman: University of Oklahoma Press, 2002, 284–315.

Baca Zinn, Maxine. "Gender and Ethnicity Among Chicanos." *Frontiers* 5 (1980): 18–23.

Barrett, Edith J. "Black Women in State Legislatures: The Relationship of Race and Gender to the Legislative Experience." In *The Impact of Women in Public Office*, edited by Susan J. Carroll, 185–204. Bloomington: Indiana University Press, 2001.

Bedolla, Lisa Garcia, Katherine Tate, and Janelle Wong. "Indelible Effects: The Impact of Women of Color in the U.S. Congress." In *Women and Elective Office: Past, Present, And Future*, edited by Sue Thomas and Clyde Wilcox. New York: Oxford University Press, 2005, 152–75.

Bledsoe, Timothy, and Mary Herring. "Victims of Circumstances: Women in Pursuit of Political Office." *American Political Science Review* 84 (1990): 213–23.

Boles, Janet. "The Texas Women in Politics: Role Model or Mirage?" *Social Science Journal* 21 (1984): 79–89.

Bratton, Kathleen A., and Kerry L. Haynie. "Agenda Setting and Legislative Success in State Legislatures: The Effects of Gender and Race." *Journal of Politics* 61 (1999): 658–79.

Brown, Lyle, Joyce Langenegger, Sonia Garcia, and Ted Lewis. *Practicing Texas Politics*. 12th ed. Boston: Houghton Mifflin, 2003.

Burrell, Barbara. "Women Candidates in Open-Seat Primaries for the U.S. House: 1968–1990." *Legislative Studies Quarterly* 17, no. 4 (1992): 493–508.

Burt-Way, Barbara, and Rita Mae Kelly. "Gender and Sustaining Political Ambition: A Study of Arizona Elected Officials." *Western Political Quarterly* 45, no. 1 (1992): 11–26.

Carroll, Susan, ed. *The Impact of Women in Public Office.* Bloomington: Indiana University Press, 2001.

———. "Representing Women: Congressmen's Perceptions of Their Representational Roles." In *Women Transforming Congress,* edited by Cindy Simon Rosenthal, 50–68. Norman: University of Oklahoma Press, 2002.

———. *Women as Candidates in American Politics.* Bloomington, Ind.: Indiana University Press, 1994.

Caul-Kittilson, Miki. "Political Parties and the Adoption of Candidate Gender Quotas: A Cross-National Analysis." *Journal of Politics* 63, no. 4 (2001): 1214–29.

Chapman, Valeria Sinclair. "Presence, Promise, and Progress: Black Representation in the U.S. Congress." Unpublished manuscript. Ohio State University, 2002.

———. "Symbols and Substance." Paper presented at the Annual Convention of the 1996 American Political Science Association, San Francisco, 1996.

Clapp, Charles. *The Congressman: His Work as He Sees It.* Garden City, N.Y.: Anchor Books, 1964.

Clark, Janet. "Women in State and Local Politics: Progress or Stalemate?" *Social Science Journal* 21 (1984): 1–4.

Clift, Eleanor, and Tom Brazaitis. *Madam President.* New York: Routledge, 2003.

Cohen, Cathy J. "A Portrait of Marginality: The Study of Women of Color in American Politics." In *Women and American Politics: New Questions, New Direction,* edited by Susan Carroll. Oxford: Oxford University Press, 2003, 190–213.

Cox, Gary W., and Matthew D. McCubbins. *Legislative Leviathan: Party Government in the House.* Berkeley: University of California Press, 1993.

Crenshaw, Kimberlè Williams. "Beyond Racism and Misogyny: Black Feminism and 2 Live Crew." In *Women Transforming Politics,* edited by Cathy Cohen, Kathy Jones, and Joan Tronto. New York: New York University Press, 1997, 549–68.

Darcy, R., Susan Welch, and Janet Clark. *Women, Elections and Representation.* 2d ed. Lincoln: University of Nebraska, 1994.

Darling, Marsha J. "African-American Women in State Elective Office in the South." In *Women And Elective Office,* edited by Sue Thomas and Clyde Wilcox, 15–62. New York: New York University Press, 1997.

Davidson, Chandler. *Race and Class in Texas Politics.* Princeton, N.J.: Princeton University Press, 1990.

DeLeon, Arnoldo. *Mexican Americans in Texas: A Brief History.* Wheeling, Ill.: Harlan Davidson, 1993.

Dickens, Edwin L. "The Political Role of Mexican Americans in San Antonio, Texas," Ph.D. diss., Texas Technical University, 1969. As cited in *A History of Mexican American and Mexican Women in San Antonio, Texas: Works, Education, and Organizational Politics, 1900–1990,* by Cynthia Orozco 77–101. San Antonio: Hispanas Unidas Research Project, 1996.

Dobson, Debra. "Representing Women's Interests in the U.S. House of Representatives." In *Women and Elective Office: Past, Present, and Future,* edited by Sue Thomas and Clyde Wilcox. New York: Oxford University Press, 1998, 129–51.

Dolan, Kathleen. *Voting for Women.* Boulder, Colo.: Westview Press, 2004.

Dolan, Kathleen, and Lynne E. Ford. "Are All Women State Legislators Alike?" In *Women and Elective Office: Past, Present, and Future,* edited by Sue Thomas and Clyde Wilcox. New York: Oxford University Press, 1998, 41–59.

Douglas, Arnold, R. *The Logic of Congressional Action.* New Haven, Conn.: Yale University Press, 1990.

Duerst-Lahti, Georgia. "Knowing Congress as a Gendered Institution: Manliness and the Implications of Women in Congress." In *Women Transforming Congress,* edited by Cindy Simon Rosenthal, 20–49. Norman: University of Oklahoma Press, 2002.

Eagly, Alice, and Blair Johnson. "Gender and Leadership Style: A MetaAnalysis," *Psychological Bulletin* 108 (1990): 233–56.

Elazar, Daniel. *American Federalism: A View from the States.* New York: Crowell, 1972.

Enloe, Cynthia. *The Curious Feminist.* Berkeley: University of California Press, 2004.

Fenno, Richard. F. Jr. *Congressmen in Committees.* Boston: Little Brown, 1973.

Fiedler, Fred. *A Theory of Leadership Effectiveness.* New York: McGraw-Hill, 1967.

Fiorina, Morris P. *Congress: Keystone of the Washington Establishment.* New Haven, Conn.: Yale University Press, 1977.

Flammang, Janet. *Political Women: Current Roles in State and Local Government.* Beverly Hills, Calif.: Sage Publications, 1984.

Fowlkes, Diane. "Ambitious Political Women: Counter Socialization and Political Party Context." *Women & Politics* 4 (1984): 5–32.

Fowlkes, Diane, Jerry Perkins, and Sue Tolleson-Rinehart. "Gender Roles and Party Roles." *American Political Science Review* 73, no. 3 (1979): 772–80.

Fraga, Luis Ricardo, and Sharon A. Navarro. "Latinas in Latino Politics."

Paper presented at conference, "Latino Politics: The State of the Discipline," Texas A&M University, College Station, Tex., April 30–May 1, 2004.

Fraga, Luis Ricardo, Valerie Martinez-Ebers, Ricardo Ramirez, and Linda Lopez. "Gender and Ethnicity: The Political Incorporation of Latina and Latino State Legislators." Paper presented at seminar, "Inequality and Social Policy," John F. Kennedy School of Government, Nov. 10, 2005.

———. "Strategic Intersectionality: Gender, Ethnicity, and Political Incorporation." Prepared for delivery at the Annual Meeting of the American Political Science Association, Washington, D.C., August 31–September 4, 2005.

Freeman, Jo. *A Room at a Time: How Women Entered Party Politics.* Lanham, Md.: Rowman and Littlefield, 2000.

———. "The Political Culture of the Democratic and Republican Parties," *Political Science Quarterly* 101, no. 3 (1986): 327–56.

Gaddie, R. K., and Charles Bullock. "Congressional Elections and the Year of the Woman: Structural and Elite Influences on Female Candidacies." *Social Science Quarterly* 76 (1995): 749–62.

———. "Structural and Elite Features in Open Seat and Special U.S. House Elections: Is There a Sexual Bias?" *Political Research Quarterly* 50, no. 2 (1997): 459–68.

Garcia, Sonia. "Empowering Women: San Antonio Style." Panel participant at the Annual Conference for the Social Science Association, San Antonio, Tex., 1997.

Garcia, Sonia. "Running as a Latina: Building a Campaign." Paper presented at the Annual Meeting of the Western Political Science Association, Los Angeles, 1998.

———. Texas Women: Leadership Roles Among Women State Legislators in the 1990s." Paper presented at the Annual Meeting of the Western Political Science Association, Las Vegas, 2001.

Garcia, Sonia, Irasema Coronado, Valerie Martinez-Ebers, Sharon A. Navarro, and Patricia Jaramillo, eds. *Políticas: Latina Trailblazers in the Texas Political Arena.* Austin: University of Texas Press, 2008.

Garcia, Sonia, and Marisela Marquez. "Motivational and Attitudinal Factors among Latinas in U.S. Electoral Politics." *NWSA Journal* 13, no. 2 (2001): 112–22.

Gertzog, Irwin. "The Routinization of Committee Assignments in the U.S. House of Representatives." *American Journal of Political Science* 20, no. 4 (1976): 693–712.

———. "Women's Changing Pathways to the U.S. House of Representatives: Widows, Elites, and Strategic Politicians." In *Women Transforming Con-*

gress, edited by Cindy Simon Rosenthal, 95–118. Norman: University of Oklahoma Press, 2002.

Gilligan, Carol. *In a Different Voice: Psychological Theory and Women's Development.* Cambridge, Mass.: Harvard University Press, 1982.

Gruberg, Martin. "From Nowhere to Where? Women in State and Local Politics." *Social Science Journal* 21 (1984): 5–12.

Guerra, Fernando. "The Emergence of Ethnic Officeholders in California." In *Racial and Ethnic Politics in California,* edited by Bryan Jackson and Michael Preston. Berkeley: University of California Press, Institute of Governmental Studies, 1991, 78–101.

Gutierrez, Jose Angel, and Rebecca E. Deen. "Chicanas in Texas Politics." Occasional Paper No. 66, Latino Studies Series. Michigan State University, Julian Samora Research Institute, 2000.

Hardy-Fanta, Carol. *Latina Politics, Latino Politics: Gender, Culture and Political Participation in Boston.* Boston: Temple Press, 1993.

———. "Latina Women and Political Consciousness: La Chispa Que Prende." In *Women Transforming Politics: An Alternative Reader,* edited by Cathy Cohen, Kathleen Jones and Joan Tronto. New York: New York Press, 1997, 223–37.

Hawkesworth, Mary. "Congressional Enactments of Race-Gender: Toward a Theory of Raced- Gendered Institutions." *APSR* 97, no.4 (2003): 529–50.

Helgesen, Sally. *The Female Advantage.* New York: Doubleday, 1990.

Hero, Rodney. *The Faces of Inequality: Social Diversity in American Politics.* Oxford: Oxford University Press, 1998.

Hero, Rodney, and Caroline Tolbert. "Latinos and Substantive Representation in the U.S. House of Representation: Direct, Indirect, or Nonexistent." *American Journal of Political Science* 39, no. 3 (1995): 640–53.

Hibbing, John R. *Congressional Careers: Contours of Life in the U.S. House of Representatives.* Chapel Hill: University of North Carolina Press, 1991.

Hill, David B. "Political Cultures and Female Political Representation." *The Journal of Politics* 43, no. 1 (1981): 159–68.

Hochschild, Arlie. *The Managed Heart: Commercialization of Human Feeling.* Berkeley: University of California Press, 1983.

Hochschild, Arlie, and Anne Machung. *The Second Shift: Working Parents and the Revolution at Home.* New York: Viking, 1989.

Institute for Women's Policy Research. *The Status of Women in Texas.* Washington, D.C.: 1996.

Jackson, Bryan, and Michael Preston, eds. *Racial and Ethnic Politics in California.* Berkeley: University of California, Institute of Governmental Studies, 1991.

Jacobson, Gary. "Strategic Politicians and the Dynamics of House Elections, 1946–86." *American Political Science Review* 83, No. 3 (1989): 773–93.

Jamieson, Kathleen Hall. *Beyond the Double Bind: Woman and Leadership.* New York: Oxford University Press, 1995.

Jewell, Malcom E., and Marcia Lynn Whicker. *Legislative Leadership in the American States.* Ann Arbor: University of Michigan Press, 1994.

Jeydel, Alana, and Andrew J. Taylor. "Are Women Legislators Less Effective? Evidence from the U.S. House in the 103rd-105th Congress." *Political Research Quarterly* 56, no.1 (2003): 19–27.

Jones, Nancy Baker, and Ruthe Winegarten. *Capitol Women: Texas Female Legislators 1923–1999.* Austin: University of Texas Press, 2000.

Kahn, Kim Fridkin. "Gender Differences in Campaign Messages: The Political Advertisement of Men and Women Candidates for the U.S. Senate." *Political Research Quarterly* 46 (1993): 481–501.

———. *The Political Consequences of Being a Woman: How Stereotypes Influence the Conduct and Consequences of Political Campaigns.* New York: Columbia University Press, 1996.

Kathleen, Lyn. "Power and Influence in State Legislative Policymaking: The Interaction of Gender and Position in Committee Hearing Debates." *American Political Science Review* 88, no. 3 (1994): 560–76.

———. "Uncovering the Political Impacts of Gender: An Exploratory Study." *Western Political Quarterly* 42, no. 2 (1989): 397–421.

Kelly, Rita Mae, and Mary Boutilier. *The Making of Political Women.* Chicago: Nelson-Hall, 1978.

Kenney, Sally J. "New Research on Gendered Political Institutions." *Political Research Quarterly* 49, no. 2 (1994): 445–66.

Kirkpatrick, Jeane. *Political Woman.* New York: Basic Books, 1974.

KLRN Public Television, "Polithon '90," Transcript, October 21, 1990.

la Cour Dabelko, Kristen, and Paul Hernson. "Women and Men's Campaigns for the U.S. House of Representatives." *Political Research Quarterly* 50 (1997): 121–35.

Lawless, Jennifer, and Richard Fox. *It Takes a Candidate: Why Women Don't Run for Office.* Cambridge: Cambridge University Press, 2005.

Little, Thomas, Dana Dunn, and Rebecca Deen. "A View From the Top: Gender Differences in Legislative Priorities Among State Legislative Leaders." *Women & Politics* 22, no. 4 (2001): 29–50.

MacManus, Susan. "Voter Participation and Turnout: It's a New Game." In *Gender and Elections,* edited by Susan Carroll and Richard Fox, 43–73. New York: Cambridge University Press, 2006.

Marquez, Marisela. "Mobilizing Change: An Examination of Latina Political Organizations." Paper presented at the annual conference of the

Western Political Science Association, Oakland, Cal., March 16–18, 2005.

Mansbridge, Jane. "Rethinking Representation." *American Political Science Review* 97, no. 4 (2003): 515–28.

———. "Should Blacks Represent Blacks and Women Represent Women? A Contingent 'Yes.'" *Journal of Politics* 61 (1999): 628–57.

Masters, Nicholas A. "Committee Assignments in the House of Representatives." *American Political Science Review* 46 (1961): 1046–55.

Matland, Richard, and David King. "Sex and the Grand Old Party." *American Politics Research* 31, no. 6 (2003): 595–612.

Maxwell, William Earl, and Ernest Crain. *Texas Politics Today.* 12th ed. Belmont, Calif.: Thomas Higher Education, 2006.

Mayhew, David R. *America's Congress: Action in the Public Sphere, James Madison Through Newt Gingrich.* New Haven, Conn.: Yale University Press, 2000.

Melville, Margarita B., ed. *Twice a Minority: Mexican American Women.* St. Louis: Mosby, 1980.

Moncrief, Gary, Joel Thompson, and Robert Schuhmann. "Gender, Race, and the State Legislature: A Research Note on the Double Disadvantage Hypothesis." *Social Science Journal* 28 (1991): 481–87.

Montoya, Lisa, Carol Hardy-Fanta, and Sonia Garcia. "Latina Politics: Gender, Participation and Leadership." *PS: Political Science and Politics* 23, no. 3 (2000): 555–62.

Moreno, Paul. Law Offices of Moreno & Briones, Attorneys at Law, 1140 Southwest National Bank Bldg., El Paso, Tex. 79901, September 27, 1974 (unpublished).

Morrow, William L. *A Republic If You Can Keep It, Constitutional Politics and Public Policy.* Upper Saddle River, N. J.: Prentice Hall, 2000.

National Association of Latino Elected and Appointed Officials. *National Directory of Latino Elected Officials,* 2005.

Navarro, Sharon. "Latina Mayors." In *Políticas: Latina Trailblazers in the Texas Political Arena,* edited by Sonia Garcia, Irasema Coronado, Valerie Martinez-Ebers, Sharon A. Navarro, and Patricia Jaramillo. Austin: University of Texas Press, 2008, 89–106.

Newman, Jody. "Perception and Reality: A Study Comparing the Success of Men and Women Candidates." Prepared for the National Women's Political Caucus, Washington, D.C., 1994.

Norris, Pippa. "The Impact of the Electoral System on Election of Women to National Legislatures." In *Different Roles, Different Voices,* edited by Marianne Githens, Pippa Norris, and Joni Lovenduski. New York: Harper Collins, 1994, 71–95.

Norris, Pippa, and Joni Lovenduski. *Political Recruitment: Gender, Race and Class in the British Parliament.* Cambridge: Cambridge University Press, 1995.

Norton, Noelle H. "Women, It's Not Enough to Be Elected: Committee Position Makes a Difference." In *Gender Power, Leadership, and Governance,* edited by Georgia Duerst-Lahti and Rita Mae Kelly. Ann Arbor: University of Michigan Press, 1995, 115–40.

Orozco, Cynthia. "Mexican American Democrats," *Handbook of Texas Online,* s.v. , http://www.tsha.utexas.edu/handbook/online/articles/MM/wmm2.html. (Accessed July 5, 2006).

Pardo, Mary. "Mexican American Grassroots Community Activists: 'Mothers of East Los Angeles.'" *Frontiers* 11, no. 1 (1990): 1–7.

Perkins, Jerry. "Political Ambition Among Black and White Women: An Intragender Test of the Socialization Model." *Women & Politics* 6, no. 1 (1986): 27–40.

Pierce, Patrick. "Gender Role and Political Cultural: The Electoral Connection." *Women & Politics* 9, no. 1 (1989): 21–46.

Pitkin, Hannah. *The Concept of Representation.* Berkeley: University of California Press, 1967.

Potter, Linda. "Women in the Texas Legislature. Seen and Heard? A Preliminary Study of Memberships and Chairships on Mega Committee." In *Texas Politics Today,* edited by William Maxwell and Ernest Crain. Los Angeles: West/Wadsworth Publishing, 1998, 214–15.

Prindeville, Diane-Michele, and Teresa Braley Gomez. "American Indian Women Leaders, Public Policy, and the Importance of Gender and Ethnic Identity." *Women & Politics* 20 (1999): 17–32.

Rodriguez, Sylvia. "Changing Political Parties: The Impact on Executives and Legislatures." Robert A. Taft Institute of Government at Queens College, Flushing, New York. July 18, 1978. (unpublished).

Rohde, David W., and Kenneth A. Shepsle. "Democratic Committee Assignments in the House of Representatives: Strategic Aspects of a Social Choice Process." *The American Political Science Review* 67, no. 3 (1973): 889–905.

Rosales, Rodolfo. *The Illusion of Inclusion: The Untold Political Story of San Antonio.* Austin: University of Texas Press, 2000.

Rosenthal, Cindy Simon. "Gender Styles in State Legislative Committees: Raising Their Voices in Resolving Conflict." *Women and Politics* 21, no. 2 (2000): 21–45.

———. *When Women Lead: Integrative Leadership in State Legislatures.* New York: Oxford University Press, 1998.

———. "Women Leading Legislature," In *Women and Elective Office,* edited by Sue Thomas and Clyde Wilcox. New York: Oxford University Press, 2005, 197–212.

Rule, Wilma. "Electoral Systems, Contextual Factors, and Women's Opportunity for Election to Parliament in Twenty-Three Democracies." *Western Political Quarterly* 40, no. 2 (1987): 477–98.

Rule, Wilma, and Pippa Norris. "Anglo and Minority Women's Underrepresentation in Congress: Is the Electoral System the Culprit?" In *United States Electoral Systems: Their Impact on Women and Minorities,* edited by Wilma Rule and Joseph F. Zimmerman. New York: Greenwood Press, 1992.

Sanbonmatsu, Kira. *Democrats, Republicans, and the Politics of Women's Place.* Ann Arbor: University of Michigan Press, 2002.

Sapiro, Virginia, and Barbara Farah. "New Pride & Old Prejudice: Political Ambition and Role Orientations Among Female Partisan Elites." *Women & Politics* 1 (1980): 13–37.

———. *The Political Integration of Women: Roles, Socialization and Politics.* Urbana: University of Illinois Press, 1983.

Schlesinger, Joseph A. *Ambition and Politics: Political Careers in the United States.* Chicago: Rand McNally, 1966.

Segura, Denise A. "Chicanas and Triple Oppression in the Labor Force." In *Chicana Voices: Intersection of Class, Race, and Gender,* edited by Teresa Cordova. Albuquerque: University of New Mexico Press, 1986, 47–65.

Seidman, Irving. *Interviewing and Qualitative Research: A Guide for Researchers in Education and the Social Sciences.* New York: Columbia University Teachers College Press, 1991.

Seligman, Lester, Michael R. Kink, and Chong Lim Kim. *Patterns of Recruitment.* Chicago: Rand McNally, 1974.

Siems, Larry. "Loretta Sanchez and the Virgin." *Aztlan: A Journal of Chicano Studies* 24, no. 1 (1999): 151–74.

Sierra, Christine, and Adaljiza Sosa-Riddell. "Chicanas as Political Actors: Rare Literature, Complex Practice." *National Political Science Review* 4 (1994): 297–317.

———. From Activist to Mayor: The Controversial Politics of Debbie Jaramillo in Santa Fe, New Mexico." Panel presentation at the Annual Meeting of the Western Political Science Association, Tucson, Ariz., 1997.

Sinclair, Barbara. "The Distribution of Committee Positions in the U.S. Senate: Explaining Institutional Change." *American Journal of Political Science* 32 (1988): 276–301.

Smith, Steven S., and Christopher J. Deering. *Committees in Congress.* Washington, D.C.: Congressional Quarterly Press, 1990.

Smooth, Wendy G. *African American Women State Legislators: The Impact of*

Gender and Race on Legislative Influence. Ph.D. diss., University of Maryland, 2001.

Sparks, Holloway. "Dissident Citizenship: Democratic Theory, Political Courage, and Activist Women." *Hypatia* 12, no. 4 (1997): 74–110.

Stanley, Jeanie R. Coleman. "Gender Politics in the 1994 Texas Election." *Texas Journal of Political Studies* 18 (1996): 4–31.

Steinberg, Ronnie J. "Gender on the Agenda: Male Advantage in Organizations." *Contemporary Sociology* 21, no. 5 (1992): 576–81.

Strauss, Anselm, and Juliet Corbin. *Basics of Qualitative Research: Techniques and Procedures for Developing Grounded Theory*. 2d ed. Thousand Oaks, Calif.: Sage Publishing, 1998.

Takash, Paule Cruz. "Breaking Barriers to Representation: Chicana/Latina Elected Officials in California." *Urban Anthropology* 22 (1993): 325–360. Reprinted in Cathy Cohen, Kathleen Jones and Joan Tronto, *Women Transforming Politics: An Alternative Reader*. New York: New York Press, 1997, 412–34.

Tamerius, Karin L. "Sex, Gender, and Leadership in the Representation of Women." In *Gender Power, Leadership, and Governance*, edited by Georgia Duest-Lahtia and Rita Mae Kelly. Ann Arbor: University of Michigan Press, 1995, 93–112.

Tate, Katherine. "Women and State Legislatures: One Step at a Time." In *The Year of the Woman: Myths and Realities*, edited by Elizabeth Adell Cook, Sue Thomas, and Clyde Wilcox. San Francisco: Westview Press, 2003, 141–60.

Thomas, Sue. *How Women Legislate*. New York: Oxford University Press, 1994.

———. "The Impact of Women on State Legislative Policies." *Journal of Politics* 53 (1991): 958–76.

Thomas, Sue, and Clyde Wilcox, eds. *Women and Elective Office: Past, Present, and Future*. New York: Oxford University Press, 2005.

Tolleson-Rinehart, Sue, and Jeanie R. Stanley. *Claytie and the Lady: Ann Richards, Gender and Politics in Texas*. Austin: University of Texas Press, 1994.

Valian, Virginia. *Why So Slow?* Cambridge, Mass.: MIT Press, 1999.

Vega, Arturo, and Juanita Firestone. "The Effects of Gender on Congressional Behavior and the Substantive Representation of Women." *Legislative Studies Quarterly* 22, no. 2 (1995): 213–22.

———. "Gender and Ethnicity Effects on the Legislative Behavior and Substantive Representation of the Texas Legislature." *Texas Journal of Political Studies* 19 (1997): 1–18.

Walsh, Katherine Cramer. "Enlarging Representation: Women Bringing

Marginalized Perspectives to Floor Debate in the House of Representatives." In *Women Transforming Congress,* edited by Cindy S. Rosenthal. Norman: University of Oklahoma Press, 2002, 370–96.

Welch, Susan, and Rebecca Herrick. "The Impact of At-Large Elections on the Representation of Minority Women." In *United States Electoral Systems: Their Impact on Women and Minorities,* edited by Wilma Rule and Joseph F. Zimmerman. New York: Greenwood Press, 1992, 153–66.

Welch, Susan, and Donley Studlar. "Multimember Districts and the Representation of Women: Evidence from Britain and the United States." *Journal of Politics* 52 (1990): 391–412.

Witt, Linda, M. Paget, and Glenna Matthews. *Running as a Woman: Gender and Power in American Politics.* New York: Free Press, 1995.

INDEX